# Wojtek the Bear

## Polish War Hero

**Aileen Orr** was born in Dumfries and raised in Lockerbie before going on to study at the London School of Economics. After a few years in banking, she married and became Regional Director of the SCA. She stood for both the Westminster and Scottish Parliament and currently enjoys working with parliamentarians on a variety of issues and all things Polish. She is currently chair of Dyslexia Scotland in the Scottish Borders.

**Neal Ascherson** was born in Edinburgh and studied at Cambridge University. A journalist for many years, he has also published numerous books and is well known as an authority on Polish and East European affairs.

# Wojtek the Bear

## Polish War Hero

### Aileen Orr

BIRLINN

*Dedicated to the memory of Augustyn Karolewski of Hutton Village, who inspired the writing of this book. He was one of the many unrecognised Poles who fought for your freedom and ours.*

This edition first published in 2014 by
Birlinn Limited
West Newington House
10 Newington Road
Edinburgh
EH9 1QS

*www.birlinn.co.uk*

Reprinted 2015

ISBN: 978 1 84341 065 2

British Library Cataloguing-in-Publication Data
A catalogue record for this book is available from the British Library

Typeset by Iolaire Typesetting, Newtonmore
Printed and bound in Italy by Grafica Veneta
www.graficaveneta.com

# CONTENTS

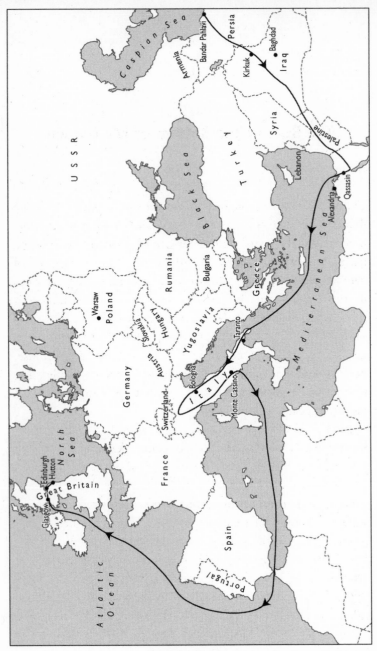

*Wojtek's Journey*

# The Bear at the Bottom of My Garden

Outside it was one of those beautiful sunny days that make living in the Scottish Borders a privilege: a somnolent summer's day with hardly a breath of wind to disturb the ripening barley and wheat that stretched out in a great expanse of patchwork fields, heavy ears of cereal drooping off their stalks in the heat. Even the vivid yellow splashes of rape – a relatively new crop on Scottish farms maintaining centuries of traditional agricultural practice – didn't overpower the gentle beauty of the scene. Beyond the red-brick farmhouse, bees bumbled around lush bushes and hedgerows collecting nectar. Sunwick Farm was, to all outward appearances, a vision of peace and tranquillity.

Indoors, the house and domestic office phones were ringing off the hook, and I was panicking like mad. Everyone wanted to talk to me about Wojtek (pronounced *Voy-check*), the Syrian brown bear that used to live at the bottom of our garden, and learn more about the memorial I intended to raise to him, although at that juncture I hadn't a clue how I was going to get the project off the ground. It had all started out innocently enough. A couple of Scottish newspapers had run articles on my idea to create a memorial for the bear who was officially made a private in the Polish army and who fought side by side with Polish troops during the Second World War before retiring to the Scottish Borders. What I had not bargained for was the way the story had been picked up by the international media. Wojtek had captured the world's imagination – or, more accurately, the vast diaspora of Polish exiles around the globe. The BBC, Good Morning Australia and news channels in New Zealand, Canada and the US had all reported that he liked a cigarette, a bottle of beer and a playful wrestle with his companions, and that a farmer's wife in Scotland wanted to commemorate his life by commissioning a statue of him.

I had always assumed that my fascination with Wojtek, which extended right through my childhood until the present day, was unique, and that apart from a few old soldiers who hadn't yet faded away I was exploring a minor, if somewhat unusual, historical cul-de-sac. I could not have been more wrong. Wojtek's appeal is universal. The legend of Wojtek has been handed down the generations by thousands of people. Deluged by e-mails and phone calls from those wanting to share their reminiscences of the bear with me, I began to suspect that, in his own ursine way, Wojtek was as popular as Elvis. And when officials at the Scottish Parliament in Edinburgh pulled me into the ministerial tower at Holyrood to inform me that a small function to celebrate Wojtek's life was being upgraded to a full-scale diplomatic reception with political dignitaries flying in from Poland, I was sure of it.

I shouldn't have been surprised. From the moment Wojtek set foot on Scottish soil he was a star. Certainly, his arrival from overseas in 1946 produced a Scottish ticker-tape welcome. His first glimpse of Scotland was Glasgow; thousands of Glaswegians lined the streets to cheer him and his Polish regiment as they marched through the city. In the grey age of postwar austerity, he must have been a considerable spectacle. His story was known to the populace and he was regarded as a war hero, so the welcome was genuine and heartfelt. The bear revelled in it.

By that time, he was, of course, a seasoned military campaigner, having spent 26 months travelling through the Middle East with his comrades, followed by a 32-month stint in Italy where he saw active service as the Allies fought their way towards the heart of Europe.

Wojtek arrived at what was then Winfield Camp for Displaced Persons on Sunwick Farm on 28 October 1946, and it wasn't long before news of his presence swept round the community. The villages of Hutton and Paxton close by ensured a steady stream of visitors and, despite rationing, food. For Wojtek, food was the most important part of his life. While he basked in the admiration of his many visitors, most of all he loved to be fed.

Right from the start Wojtek won a place in Scotland's heart. It's also readily understandable why the Polish servicemen held him so dear. Far from home, the bear provided entertainment and fun. He was the child they had left behind, the pet dog they had loved. The day-to-day challenges of feeding him and keeping him occupied also distracted them from the horrors of war, a war that had inflicted unspeakable atrocities and hardships on Poland. At Winfield Camp Wojtek's ambling presence, a free spirit, lifted the hearts of many men whose future appeared to be non-existent. It banished, if only temporarily, some of the men's anxieties about the future and gave them a glimpse of the joy of an uncomplicated existence.

In truth, the life of a displaced person in Scotland in the postwar years was always a mixture of homesickness and fear. The Poles nursed unimaginable emotional pain without ever revealing it to the Scots around them. They came from a country which in September 1939 had been caught between the devil and the deep blue sea – Poland was divided between Russia and Germany in a secret pact between the two major powers. The cruelty of both invaders knew no bounds.

After subjugating Poland in a few brief weeks the Nazis went on to make it a killing field, establishing six extermination camps on Polish soil including Auschwitz and Treblinka. In these two death camps alone the Germans murdered at least 2 million people, including Poles.

Meanwhile, East Poland felt the lash of cruel enslavement by Russia's Red Army and their *apparatchiks*. In February 1940, Stalin's ethnic cleansing began in earnest. Men, women and children were rounded up and forced onto railway cattle trucks and transported into the secret and inconceivably terrifying depths of Stalin's Russia. One in twelve of the deported Poles were sent to gulags in Siberia. It is estimated a total of 1.5 million Poles from the Soviet zone were sent to Russian camps. Only a tenth of this number would emerge alive less than two years later, including more than 100,000 fighting men; when Germany invaded Russia in 1941 the Poles' repatriation was the price Stalin grudgingly had to pay to join the Allies.

At Winfield Camp, many of Wojtek's companions from East Poland were among the number freed from Siberia in 1941. Having experienced Sovietisation at first hand, many Poles had no wish, ever again, to place themselves at the mercy of Stalin's regime.

In later years many Poles would focus their grief and rage on single atrocities which became an emotional touchstone, a sort of hideous shorthand that encompassed all that they had suffered and lost in terms of families, loved ones, homes and occupations. The Katyn Forest massacre is one such atrocity, which was based on a secret death list drawn up by Lavrentiy Beria, Stalin's security chief, and intended to rip out Poland's intellectual heart. An estimated 22,000 Polish military officers, policemen, intellectuals and civilian POWs were murdered. Only approximately 4,400 Katyn victims have ever been identified. In 1943 the Nazis exhumed the Polish dead and blamed the Soviets. In 1944, having retaken the Katyn area from the Nazis, in a macabre exercise of grisly political oneupmanship, the Soviets again exhumed the Polish dead and blamed the Nazis for the massacre. Some eight other known death sites still have not been excavated.

There is considerable controversy over how much the Allies knew about the Katyn massacre before 1991, when Soviet documents were found that proved Stalin had ordered the killings. In the war years many Poles believed Allied governments colluded in keeping silent about the Soviet involvement because it would have upset other political considerations. These suspicions were never publicly voiced, of course. In a bizarre and tragic twist, on 10 April 2010 a plane carrying the Polish president Lech Kaczynski and Poland's entire military leadership crashed near Smolensk in Russia killing all 96 people on board. The president, along with his wife Maria and former president Ryszard Kaczor-owkski were travelling with the many prominent Polish dignitaries from Warsaw to attend the 70th anniversary of the massacre in Katyn forest. Sadly, amongst the passengers were relatives of the victims, adding to the pathos and pain of one of the many atrocities of the war in Europe. The only positive outcome of the crash was the declassification of restricted documents relating to Katyn by Russia as well as a full and frank statement admitting Stalin did in fact person-ally order the Katyn massacre. Winfield Camp's Polish servicemen were remarkably tight-lipped about such matters. 'You have to remember that your country took us in and allowed us to stay. You were our friends,' I was told by one former Winfield Camp serviceman, now in his 80s.

A Scottish acquaintance told me that he and that same Winfield Camp serviceman had visited the Pole's homeland in

Silesia. As they walked through his native village, the service-man pointed to a cemetery on one side of the road. 'That's the German cemetery,' he said. 'That's where they executed many of the village's young men, including my brother.' A few hundred yards further on the two reached another graveyard and he said: 'That's the Russian cemetery. That's where the Russians shot my other brother in their mass executions.'

I had known the Polish serviceman for more than 30 years and he had never once hinted at the annihilation of his family. When I challenged him about it he said simply: 'These are things I do not like to think about.'

The memory of these atrocities was silently endured by the Poles who came to Scotland and, hopefully, a new life. Scotland was the arrival point for many Polish servicemen brought to the UK before being dispersed to camps across Britain. They would barely be settled into one camp before being moved on to another. Tens of thousands finally ended their travels at Winfield or at the many other camps in the Borders, Fife and other parts of Scotland. It was a very confusing time for them.

A lot of the men at Winfield, when they got there, had only a hazy idea of where they were. Large numbers of them were illiterate, having had no formal schooling, so they were unable to write to their families to tell them they were safe. Being unable to read or write in Polish, they were effectively cut off from their loved ones. That sense of intense isolation was compounded by another cruel quirk of fate. In the camps many men did learn to read and write – but in English, not Polish. Thus they spoke Polish, but could not read or write in their native language. It was a strange, convoluted situation created by wartime.

Living in limbo, as they were, Wojtek's presence did much

to lift their spirits. In 1946, billeted in postwar rural Scotland, they were stateless, homeless and penniless; the only things they owned were a few meagre possessions in a bag – and a bear.

In other parts of the country, such as the west of Scotland, where the religious divide between Protestant and Roman Catholic was a long-running problem, there was a certain reserve between Polish incomers and locals. However, living in displaced persons camps, the Poles were largely out of sight, if not out of mind, and they didn't impinge too greatly on local sensibilities.

In the Borders, attitudes were different. There were few Roman Catholic churches in the area so Masses were held at the camp by visiting priests. But Winfield Camp was located among a farming community, and if there is one thing that commands universal respect in agricultural societies, it is hard physical work. Our new Polish neighbours were good workers. Many of the servicemen came from an agricultural background. They were exceptionally good at working with horses, although they had difficulty in fathoming the completely different way that harnesses were fastened in Scotland. They were also skilled at leatherwork – fast vanishing in agricultural Scotland even then – and were adept at mending harnesses.

While the Poles offered the local population agricultural skills and a willingness to work, the bear offered friendship and joy. Being country-bred, no one – adult or child – had few ordinary domestic pets. Around farms, all animals were required to earn their keep. There was no sentimentality about them. If a dog was too old to work, or took fits, it was put down.

As a child, I had experience of how creatures from the wild could be brought to accept a human environment and tamed, if only briefly. Indeed, it was something of a school sport, like marbles and conkers: every year, during the breeding season, my school pals and I would catch young jackdaws, having tracked them down to their nests in rabbit burrows. When they were half-grown but couldn't yet fly, we would remove them from their nests and put them in cardboard boxes, usually old shoeboxes, with air holes punched through the top. Then we would hand-feed the chicks worms, grubs and scraps.

In a remarkably short time, we were able to go cycling with the young birds perched on our bike handlebars, enjoying the air fluttering through their feathers. Within a month or so the jackdaws' pinion feathers would grow in and strengthen and when that happened, with their newfound maturity, they became restless. So off they flew. The pet jackdaw season was over, to be replaced by the next childhood pastime.

Wojtek, of course, was in a different category. He was an ambassador for his Polish friends, and forged links with the Borders community. But he was also an animal unique in the annals of warfare. He had never ever been trained for any of the tasks he had carried out voluntarily with his companions under shot and shell; he considered himself their equal in all respects, and had just helped out when the notion took him. That was a very strange state of affairs for an essentially wild animal, and ran contrary to the accepted opinions of many animal behaviourists. It was not thought possible for a bear to be imprinted with 'human' characteristics. Yet in terms of temperament and personality, Wojtek was very much an amalgam of both.

It was Wojtek who drove me to research the role of animals in warfare. Probably the first animals to be so employed were elephants. Their use in battle is recorded in Sanskrit writings found in the Indus Valley dating back to around 1100 BC. War elephants were deployed like tanks in battles throughout India. The slimmed-down basic 'model' would have only a mahout aboard its neck, guiding it into goring and trampling the enemy. More elaborate usage saw the war elephants equipped with armoured breastplates and headgear. Some elephants wore clanging bells or had spears attached to their tusks and others had a military-style howdah strapped to their backs, filled with warriors who rained down arrows and spears on the luckless combatants below.

The 'technology' was soon exported to other countries and used to considerable effect. For many centuries the war elephant was probably the most effective fighting machine available and its military value did not diminish until new weaponry, in the shape of the cannon, arrived on the battle-fields of India.

In more modern times many other animals have been trained to participate in warfare, including mules, horses, dogs, camels, pigeons, canaries, dolphins and sea lions. Millions of them died in the service of their country. In the First World War, even the tiny glow-worm was pressed into service in the fetid trenches of France. Soldiers used them to read their maps in the darkness.

Horses made the greatest sacrifices in the military lunacies of the First World War which saw cavalry charges against embedded machine guns persist until as late as 1918. The generals were as profligate with their animals as they were with their troops. It has been estimated that some 8 million horses died in the First World War. They did not all perish in the pointless carnage of cavalry charges, of course. The majority died bringing supplies to the front because they were deemed more reliable than mechanised transport and required relatively little maintenance. Quite a lot received no maintenance at all. They starved to death because there were no rations for them. Tens of thousands died of exposure while many more succumbed to disease and injury.

Dogs, too, were an essential part of the war effort. They were used as runners, carrying messages from the front line back through the enormous web of trenches to army headquarters. Demand for messenger dogs became so great that every police force in the UK was ordered to send strays to the War Dog Training School and the public was encouraged to donate its own pets for training – which they did in very large numbers. They were known by the troops as 'summer dogs': 'summer this' and 'summer that'. In the Second World War dogs were trained by Britain in a completely new and more sophisticated direction: they were parachuted behind enemy lines, with their handlers, on rescue missions. Their job was to sniff out explosives and find personnel trapped in the rubble of bombed buildings.

Today dogs are again being used in missions in Iraq and Afghanistan against rebel forces. Wearing specially designed oxygen masks, German shepherds are trained to parachute from 25,000 feet, strapped to SAS assault teams, in what are known as High Altitude High Opening jumps. With their handlers, they make their jumps up to 20 miles distant from their target and drift towards it. Their descents can take up to 30 minutes and at night they are practically undetectable by ground forces. On the ground, wearing mini cameras strapped to their heads, the dogs seek out insurgents' hiding places and possible booby traps.

In this age of hyper-communication, it seems barely credible that in both First and Second World Wars military strategists placed their trust in homing pigeons. But they did, either as the principal method of getting military intelligence from the front, or as a back-up to often-difficult radio communication. In fact, in the United Kingdom, there were strict Defence of the Realm regulations against shooting homing pigeons. Public posters stated sternly:

> Killing, wounding or molesting homing pigeons is punishable under the Defence of the Realm Regulations by Six Months' Imprisonment or a £100 Fine.
>
> The public are reminded that homing pigeons are doing valuable work for the government, and are requested to assist in the suppression of the shooting of these birds.
>
> £5 Reward will be paid by the National Homing Union for information leading to the conviction of any person SHOOTING HOMING PIGEONS the property of its members.

Pigeons in World War II saved many servicemen's lives by getting through to their lofts with vital SOS messages from downed aircraft in often appalling weather conditions.

On land, in the air and below the sea, it has to be said that military scientists have been dark geniuses in deploying the world's most intelligent creatures in warfare. If the 'flying dog' missions in Iraq and Afghanistan seem the stuff of a Tom Clancy techno-thriller, the US navy's intensive research into aquatic war roles for cetaceans borders on science fiction.

Since the 1950s, when military research began in earnest, dolphins, sea lions and even whales have been deployed in naval warfare. Although much of its research remains classified, it is known that between 1960 and 1990, some 240 dolphins were employed by the US navy. During the Cold War the Russians had a similar cetaceans programme. Both dolphins and sea lions have been used for a wide variety of tasks including protecting ports and navy assets from underwater attack and 'patrolling' shallow-water shipping, harbours and coastal military assets. Sea lions routinely assist in the recovery of American naval hardware such as highly expensive training targets by locating them and attaching them to recovery equipment, often diving down to depths of 500 feet.

What the foregoing shows is that, in going to war, Wojtek seemed merely to be following in the footsteps of a long line of highly courageous animals stretching back more than 3,000 years. However, there was one vital difference. Unlike these animals, Wojtek had never been trained in any aspect of warfare. He was exposed to the sound of prolonged heavy artillery barrages – both incoming and outgoing – without ever having been acclimatised to the incessant noise and the lightning-like explosions of heavy ordnance that shook the ground and sent up huge clouds of earth. Such heavy bombardments could drive even veteran troops to the verge of collapse, known then as shellshock. That Wojtek survived mentally unscathed speaks volumes about his character, and for those around him.

Wojtek died in 1963 but he continues to be a power for good. On the international front, his popularity is on the up. The Wojtek Memorial Trust launched in September 2008. Its aims – which I'll outline in more detail in a later chapter – are to promote educational links and scholarships between the young people of Scotland and Poland, and, on a broader front, to encourage new and permanent friendships between the peoples of our two nations.

That is very much as it should be. The influx of Polish workers to Scotland in recent years is really a continuation of history. The lives of Scots and Poles have been heavily entwined down the centuries. Few Scots today know that back in the seventeenth century, between 40,000 and 90,000 of our kinsfolk emigrated to Poland in search of religious freedom as well as economic betterment of their lives. The religious persecution known across Europe during the Pro-testant Reformation didn't reach Poland. In fact, religious freedom was enshrined in Polish law, making the country a beacon of civilisation in those turbulent times. And let us not forget that Bonnie Prince Charlie was half Polish – his mother was Princess Clementina Sobiesky.

Because Wojtek is involved, in the years to come the Trust will doubtless inspire some unusual projects which will make us all smile and generally stop us from taking life too seriously. After all, a charitable trust whose patron is a pint-swilling, cigarette-smoking bear who would happily wrestle anyone game enough to tangle with him, can't really be too precious about its activities.

# 2

## Love at First Sight

I must have been around eight years old when I first saw Wojtek. I can still see him, sitting on a pile of rocks behind a deep pool waving one massive paw. I was thrilled to the very bottom of my being.

A lifelong love affair was born. Let's face it, I was a pushover: an impressionable young girl, an only child, the centre of my own universe. Of course the bear was waving to me – and me alone. I had no inkling that he was a crafty old showbiz trouper who, when he wanted a bit of attention, and more probably a bit of grub, would put on a performance worthy of a film actor.

By this time Wojtek was being cared for in Edinburgh Zoo. As I clambered up the steep path to his enclosure, I was curious to see the bear I'd heard so much about. Oddly enough, on this first visit to see him, I wasn't with my grandfather, Jim Little, my great co-conspirator who used to whisk me off on travels to destinations like Moffat where there was always an ice cream or a bag of sweets at the end of the journey. This time I was with a Sunday School trip from Trinity Church in Lockerbie. There must have been 40 or 50 of us excitable youngsters who, at the zoo gates, poured off two single-decker buses, the limp remnants of coloured streamers still dangling from every window. Those streamers seldom survived any journey intact and they announced to every passer-by that this was our much-looked-forward-to annual outing.

As for me, that first Sunday School trip was unforgettable. Love at first sight always is! Be still my girlish heart, out of all the youngsters chattering and carrying on outside his enclosure, Wojtek had singled me out and waved to me. Nothing would convince me otherwise.

My grandfather had started telling me stories about Wojtek when I was quite small, probably around three years of age. Jim enjoyed my company as I was always a very inquisitive child. A soldier in his day, he had a unique view of the world which he was more than happy to share with me. Although I knew from all Jim's tales that Wojtek was a very large bear, it was only when I saw him in the flesh that I realised just how big he was. I was awestruck by his long nose and huge feet.

I always thought of Wojtek as my grandfather's bear. Indeed, when he heard that our Sunday School trip was to Edinburgh Zoo my grandfather taught me the Polish word for 'hello'. Sure enough, when I shouted it out, Wojtek immediately looked in my direction – he responded instantly whenever he heard Polish being spoken – and gave me that first wave of his large paw. Accompanying me on the trip was my classmate Renee, who was the only child of a Polish couple in the town. Their story was a mystery, their English poor, but Renee spoke fluent Polish and she laughed at my attempts to speak to Wojtek. She spoke to him at length and he sat up listening intently, his small ears twitching. Although an old bear now, he still had a sparkle. I said to Renee, 'Ask him if he remembers my grandpa,' and she did. After what seemed like an hour, she retorted, 'Yes, he does!' We were both ecstatic. The thought of it still thrills me today.

One of my ambitions, drawn from that day, is to have a plaque commemorating his life mounted at Edinburgh Zoo. When he was resident in the zoo there used to be one. But today there is no reference to him having lived there, simply due to the passage of time. He died, after all, in 1963. The world moves on and memories fade. However, nearly 50 years on, Wojtek is once more coming out of hibernation. There is international interest in his story. It is perhaps now time for his place in history to be remembered in the zoo where he spent so much of his adult life.

There were to be later visits to Wojtek in Edinburgh Zoo with my mother and my grandmother, but I recall one other overriding emotion from that first trip: I felt desperately sorry for Wojtek. In the confines of his zoo enclosure, to me, he truly looked a displaced bear. Around the farm and the camp he'd been allowed to roam free. Yes, he was locked up at night, but that was no more than happened to the other livestock. In the morning they were all let out in the fields. There is a certain sad irony about that fact: a bear in a DP (displaced persons) camp had more freedom than he did as a civilian bear living in his own compound at the zoo.

A huge admirer of the Poles' hardiness and fighting qualities, Jim visited Winfield Camp several times a week and he listened to all their tales. He always had a small treat for the bear, in the shape of an apple or some other titbit, in his pocket. It was only much later, when I began researching Wojtek's life, that memories came flooding back and I realised just how many stories Jim had told me about Wojtek.

My grandfather and Wojtek were great friends. There was a strong bond between them. In their own ways, they were both loners who had made the military their family. Wojtek had joined the Polish army as a scruffy little motherless bear cub. My grandfather, one of a family of nine, had run away from home at the age of 14 to go soldiering round the world. Fiercely independent, he was a small, wiry, bantam-cock of a man who was handy with his fists and didn't take kindly to people taking liberties. He used to be a lightweight boxer.

Like Wojtek with his Polish companions, Jim had travelled to many foreign outposts with his regiment, the King's Own Scottish Borderers, and had participated in many of the darker moments of its military engagements. As a girl I rifled through a biscuit tin in the bedroom wardrobe of Jim's home in Moniaive to sneak a peek at some of the mementos he'd brought back from foreign parts. They included photographs from the Boxer Rebellion in China when an international military force had to be sent in to rescue Westerners besieged in mission compounds by hordes of Chinese rebels. In horrid fascination I found myself staring at severed heads lying in the street where people had been executed by mobs intent on ridding China of 'foreign devils'.

In passing, it should be said that all Borderers have an abiding affection for the King's Own Scottish Borderers. Raised in 1689 to defend Edinburgh against the Jacobites, the Kosbies, as the regiment is often called by the general public (but never by the soldiers themselves), has a long and illustrious history. Still traditionally recruiting from Dumfries and Galloway, Lanarkshire and the Borders, it has served in many campaigns including the Napoleonic Wars, both World Wars and the Gulf War. There are six Victoria Crosses among its soldiers. In August 2006, despite a groundswell of protest, the regiment was amalgamated with the Royal Scots to form the Royal Scots Borderers and became the 1st Battalion Royal Regiment of Scotland.

In the KOSB my grandfather achieved the rank of colour sergeant and was a strict disciplinarian with his men. When his regiment was back in Scotland and the men were returning to their barracks in Berwick upon Tweed after being out on military manoeuvres, he would first have them run up Halidon Hill and then double-time them across to Winfield Camp at Sunwick to have a brew with Wojtek. It was a social cuppa that both the squaddies and the bear enjoyed greatly. There can't have been many farms in Scotland where you would come across a man talking over the fence to a bear which appeared to be hanging on his every word. But Sunwick was one of them.

Well before Wojtek's arrival in Berwickshire, Polish soldiers had arrived in large numbers in many of the towns and villages along the Scottish Borders. In 1942 they came to the pleasant and peaceful town of Duns. Whereas some troops had received a lukewarm welcome when passing through, Duns did the Polish troops proud. The cheers of the townsfolk were tinged with more than a little relief. Earlier, when the Poles' tanks and heavy artillery were first seen on the horizon, there had been a local scare that Duns was being invaded by enemy forces. When it was discovered the new troops were Poles, the flags on the street came out in earnest.

Younger generations have little notion of the huge number of people that moved in great waves through Scotland during and immediately after the war. Many were military personnel sent to the oddest corners of the country in strategic deployments against the German juggernaut. Tens of thousands of soldiers were bivouacked in normally sparsely populated areas of countryside. The military equivalent of fully fledged townships would spring up in fields virtually overnight, like mushrooms. It meant a tremendous influx of people into rural areas, and the Borders was no exception.

During the war years a large contingent of Polish soldiers lived in camps in nearby Symington and Douglas. They were under the charge of General Stanisław Maczek who was impressed by the warm reception from local communities. But then news of the Poles' courage and tenacity in battle had reached Scotland long before the men, so the Scots already knew the value of those soldiers as allies.

A legendary commander, respected by friend and foe alike, General Maczek led the only Polish units not to lose a single battle after Poland was invaded by the Germans in 1939. Under blitzkreig attack, his forces made a dogged defence but their efforts were eclipsed when Russia invaded from the rear and they were forced to withdraw. Maczek was loved by his soldiers, who called him *Baca*, a Galician name for a shepherd, not dissimilar from the Scottish Gaelic word, *Buachaille*.

When Germany finally capitulated, General Maczek went on to become commanding officer of all Polish forces in the United Kingdom until their demobilisation in 1947. After the war he chose to remain in Scotland, a de Gaulle-like figure who epitomised the struggle for a free Poland. Like many other Polish soldiers, he felt unable to return to Poland under the Soviet regime.

My own father had been a young pilot based at East Fortune near Edinburgh. After leaving the RAF he joined the police force in Dumfries and Galloway, and in later life spent some time at the police training college at Tulliallan Castle in Fife. He often spoke of the room, still in the college, which the Free Polish Army used as their headquarters during the war. The castle sits high looking over the narrowing Forth estuary, and few still know of the Polish secret within its walls.

The thousands of Polish servicemen left their mark on the Scottish Borders in many ways. Some stayed and created new lives and new families. One of their most enduring gifts was the open air map of Scotland they built in the grounds of what is now the Barony Castle Hotel in Eddleston, Peebleshire. While fighting in Holland, General Maczek once had been shown an impressive outdoor map of land and water in the Netherlands, demonstrating the working of the waterways which had proved such an obstacle to the Polish forces' progress in 1944. At Eddleston the general and his fellow

exiles decided to replicate the map; they conceived the Great
Polish Map of Scotland as a permanent, open-air, three-
dimensional reminder of Scotland's hospitality to their com-
patriots. In 1975 the coastline and relief map of Scotland were
laid out precisely by Kazimierz Trafas, a young geography
student from the Jagiellonian University of Kraków. An
infrastructure was built to surround it with a 'sea' of water
and, at the general's request, a number of Scotland's main
rivers on the map were even arranged to flow from head-
waters pumped into the interiors of its mountains. It was, and
still is, an amazing feat of engineering and design.

Sadly, it was allowed to fall into disrepair. After long years
of dereliction, the first steps are now being taken towards its
restoration. One day soon people will again marvel at General
Maczek's Great Polish Map of Scotland in the grounds of
Barony Castle, once the home of the Murrays of Elibank, and
later the Black Barony Hotel. In the war years the house and
grounds seem to have been in use by Polish forces, and even
then an outdoor outline map was one of the features used to
help plan the defence of the Scottish coastline which was
under threat of invasion after the fall of Norway. Whether this
was really the case, I have not been able to ascertain. Returned
to commercial use in the late 1940s, years later the hotel came
into the possession of a member of the Polish community
who had been billeted there in wartime. He was a great friend
of the general, and gave him permanent use of a suite in the
hotel. The rooms were clearly marked with Polish insignias in
plaster above the little windows.

General Maczek never did return to live in his beloved
Poland; by the time it achieved genuine freedom, age and
infirmity had taken their toll. In his later years he lived in
Edinburgh. He died in 1994 at the age of 102, his name still
synonymous with the history of World War II.

It was at the Biggar Museum that I learned much of the foregoing, as well as being made aware of the long-standing Scottish–Polish historical links which stretch back over the centuries. The town of Nowa Szkocja (Nova Scotia), for example, was named by Scots who settled in Poland in 1676. Indeed, Scots became so integrated that one of them, Alexander Czamer (Chalmers) was elected mayor of Warsaw four times before his death in 1703; sadly his tomb, housed in the Cathedral of St John in the city, was destroyed during the Warsaw uprising in 1944.

So it was of some significance when on 16 November 2008 Linda Fabiani MSP, along with organiser Paul Gogolinski, unveiled a plaque to Aleksander Czamer. In addition to his role as mayor, Czamer was also a judge and close to royalty. Paul Gogolinski, I am glad to say, is one of our esteemed Friends of Wojtek and works tirelessly to promote our links between Scotland and Poland.

With its own centuries-long history of military recruitment, the Borders took wartime upheaval pretty much in its stride. Winfield was a prime example. At the height of its use during the war years, Winfield Camp grew to a size where it accommodated 3,500 men – this in an area where the nearest villages could muster only a few hundred locals and a handful of able-bodied young men left behind in reserved occupations.

In the war years, bonded by a common purpose, and intent on keeping invaders at bay, there were relatively few strains and stresses. But when Germany surrendered and the euphoria of VE Day had dissipated, the Borders folk, in common with the rest of Scotland, began waking up to the fact that they were living in an all but bankrupt nation whose infrastructure was seriously impaired, if not wrecked; and whose social order had been changed out of all recognition. Adding to that, they had on their doorstep large numbers of refugees with no homes and indeed no country to return to, it having been bargained away like poker chips as the great powers hastily redrew the map of Europe.

In the aftermath of the war, the talk of building a land fit for heroes was paid considerable lip service. But away from the rhetoric the population imbalances and social strains could easily have overwhelmed the Borders. The bear living at the bottom of our garden would bring together two very different communities, providing each with the stimulus they needed to forge lasting ties of friendship. You might call it the Wojtek Factor.

To understand why and how it happened we have to go back to the beginning.

# 3

# Fate Takes a Hand in the Life of a Bear Cub

Sometimes life is most mysterious. It takes only a small, apparently insignificant event to pivot a life onto a completely different path – like missing your lift to work and then meeting your future husband on the next bus. The Spanish have a lovely proverb about such random events that change everything: 'God writes straight in crooked lines.'

So it was for Wojtek. By sheer good fortune, he was saved from the worst fate imaginable – life as a dancing bear.

It was April 1942, the tail-end of winter in the highlands of Iran. Despite the sunshine, the wind was still tinged with the snowy breath of the Zagros Mountains. A few hours earlier the military convoy had passed by the 4,000-year-old city of Hamadan, one of the most ancient cities in the world, and had begun the steady climb into a province of long, harsh winters and short, pleasantly cool summers.

This particular contingent of men, women and children was slowly wending its way towards Palestine, the mustering point for the 2nd Polish Corps being created and armed there. Although they didn't know it yet, they were eventually to become its 22nd Company, Polish Army Service Corps (Artillery). The convoy had stopped at the roadside for some food, a brew-up and a chance for the soldiers to stretch their legs. It was uncomfortable sitting for hour after hour on the hard, narrow seats of army lorries as they bumped and jolted their way along the rough, potholed roads of the remote uplands. However, these Poles had no complaints; this stop-and-start slow journey was like a holiday to them after enduring the privations of Siberian work camps, and besides, as the Scots saying has it: 'When you're marching you're no' fighting.'

As ever, no matter how empty the Persian landscape appeared, their passage had not gone unnoticed. In that barren spot, from out of nowhere, a barefoot young boy appeared carrying a hessian sack. He looked like so many of the half-starved youngsters the Poles had seen on their journey along the western side of the Caspian Sea – skin and bones, with enormous brown eyes in a pinched, undernourished face that had timidity and hope written over it in equal measure. In his grubby burnous the Poles supposed he was a shepherd lad from the village they had passed several miles back. Unblinking, he stared at the foreigners, watching every bite they took. The group recognised the signs; they had known it themselves. The boy was starving. They beckoned him over.

When his initial hunger had been assuaged the boy began to relax. The young Poles looked curiously at the sack tied around his neck, which appeared to be moving. Pointing at it, he pantomimed the question: what is in the sack? The boy replied in a dialect which no one understood. To everyone's immense surprise, when they cautiously loosened the bag's ties, the small black snout of a bear cub pushed out. The men gently lifted him out to get a better look. He was a scrawny, unkempt little thing, obviously not properly fed, but there was something about this defenceless, woebegone creature, no more than a few months old, that was immensely appealing.

Through sign language the inquisitive Poles asked the boy where he had got the bear. Slowly they winnowed out the story: hunters had killed the bear's mother and the boy had found the cub abandoned in a cave close by its den. It is much more likely, however, that after shooting the she-bear the hunters had actually taken her cub and given it to the boy to look after. That was how things were done in that part of the world. What the boy didn't tell them, because it was too difficult to do so, was that the little bear's future was already mapped out, and it was one of pain, torment and misery. In the culture of the region, if he survived to adulthood, which was far from being a certainty, he would become a dancing bear.

Right across the Middle East, dancing bears in the street were a commonplace sight at souks, fairs and entertainments, and were popular with children and adults alike. But few enjoying their antics had any concept of the cruelty involved in their training and of their lack of proper care. There was probably no animal more neglected and abused in the name of so-called street entertainment.

Captured from the wild and their mothers usually slaughtered, the hunters would sell on cubs like Wojtek to owners who hoped to make a living out of them. When partially grown, the bears first, without benefit of anaesthetic, had a hole pierced through either the sensitive septum of their noses, their mouths or even their palates, through which either a metal chain or rope was introduced. Trained with these restraints in a most cruel manner, the bears were forced to stand upright until they would do so on command or in response to a goad. Often the roughness of the chains or ropes caused sores and constant pain, as did the coarse edges of muzzles made for the bears out of poorly cured leather. In many instances the bears had also been declawed.

But perhaps the worst aspect of it all was that there was no good living to be earned out of street bears. Their handlers made only a few coins a day; barely enough to buy themselves enough food to eat, never mind properly feed their unfortunate charges. As a result of near constant malnutrition, poor quartering and lack of any medical care, the bears' health rapidly deteriorated. Indeed, many went blind from vitamin deficiency, and even more went mad. The lucky ones died young.

Before we start congratulating ourselves that here in Scotland we are a more humane and less primitive society, it should be noted that the dancing bears whose lives started out in the Middle East and the Balkans were regular entertainments at Highland and agricultural shows across Scotland right up until the 1960s. In the Assembly Rooms at Dumfries there is a large sepia photographic print of a giant bear standing in Dumfries High Street with its minder, a small foreign man with a short stick in his hand. The bear is on a chain and is wearing a muzzle. Judging by the models of the cars in the street, the photograph was taken around the 1930s. I have always detested the picture.

That, then, was the fate that awaited the scruffy little bear being fondled and stroked by Irena Bokiewicz and her companions as they debated whether to buy him. Roadside bartering was a way of life for the convoy. Whenever they stopped at villages small crowds would congregate, trying to sell them dried and fresh fruit, cheese, milk and anything else the hungry travellers wanted. At some villages local artisans would make them up metal pots and other implements to order, on the spot, in return for cash. They always wanted US dollars, whenever possible, because it was a much stronger currency than their own.

The boy, despite his youth, was no different. He indicated he was prepared to sell them the bear cub for dollars. But neither Irena nor her friends had any in their possession. They clubbed together to offer him some local currency and a few other goods, including a bar of chocolate and even a Swiss army knife. The boy looked doubtful, so the Poles flung in what turned out to be the deal clincher – a large tin of bully beef (better known to us as corned beef; the name 'bully beef' is a corruption of the French term for tinned boiled beef, *bœuf bouilli*).

Quickly the boy gathered up his booty, placed it in his sack, and vanished as mysteriously as he had arrived. Why he sold the bear to them, rather than await a better offer – which he would undoubtedly have had through trading him as a performing bear – no one knows. Perhaps he had difficulty finding food for him; or perhaps he thought the cub was going to die anyway. A friend of Peter's said to me, years later, of that strange transaction: 'It was the bully beef that swung it. Peter always told me that. He said the boy wasn't going to sell until the bully beef was added.'

The Polish youths looked at each other and grinned. They had acted completely on impulse, without a thought for the consequences. They now owned a bear cub. Oh, yes. Just what was needed in the middle of a world war. The officers would go off the deep end when they found out about the bear. So, naturally, they did what any self-respecting soldier the world over would have done: they didn't tell.

What on earth possessed them to buy the bear is open to numerous interpretations. Of course, the little cub was cute and its utterly vulnerable state engendered instant sympathy. It had been ripped from its natural existence and propelled into a completely alien lifestyle, so the bear and the Poles shared a common plight. But I believe the explanation is a lot simpler: the youngsters needed something to love. By the time they had discovered, through trial and error, that the cub didn't eat meat yet and was a furry fiend for diluted condensed milk fed to him via an old vodka bottle with a piece of rag in the neck

acting as a teat, they were emotionally committed and tossing
around names.

After a brisk discussion, they came up with Wojtek; it was
an apt choice. The pet name of the Polish *Wojciech*, it meant
'happy soldier' or 'happy warrior'.

By common consent, Peter Prendys was appointed Wojtek's principal guardian, a role he accepted without protest.
Aged 46, Peter was considerably older than the rest of his
comrades, many of whom were in their late teens or early
twenties. Born in 1895, he was very probably the oldest
soldier in the company. That age difference brought with it a
lot of respect and quiet authority. He certainly would have
had the confidence and experience to handle the bear cub
and, just as crucially, the patience. In army records held by the
Polish Institute and Sikorski Museum, London, it was noted
that Peter could read and write. This was a matter of some
importance, because many of the soldiers were intelligent but
semi-literate or had missed out entirely on formal education;
they were a lost generation. In the area from which most of
them came, much of the literate and intellectual classes had
been eradicated or removed. Thus, those who were teachers
or had some level of book learning were greatly prized among
the Poles. Being able to read and write made Peter a much-
sought-after non-commissioned officer. He was the man who
wrote and read letters for many of his comrades.

Despite his self-effacing manner, Peter had a quiet authority
about him and the men looked up to him. However, even
that status didn't save him from run-ins with senior officers. It
took just two days before he encountered his first bear crisis:
Wojtek's presence in the convoy was discovered.

Not that it took any great detective work. Out in the open,
and alarmed by a large and predatory-looking bird circling
above him, the cub scampered back to the safety of Peter's

truck, and ran slap-bang into the arms of the company sergeant who was on his morning tour of inspection. As the soldiers anxiously gabbled an explanation, Wojtek worked his magic. The sergeant instantly fell under the spell of the little bear and, being a good-hearted fellow, he promised to keep the men's secret until an appropriate moment arose for him to tell the commanding officer that they had an additional passenger on the trip.

They needn't have worried about the outcome. When the commanding officer, Major Chelminski, finally met Wojtek he was very taken with the little chap and for several weeks even let him sleep overnight in his tent in a portable wash basin. These sleeping arrangements continued until a small tent was eventually made available for Peter and all his new friends, and his new charge. It was an extraordinary concession for an NCO to be given his own personal quarters, but Major Chelminski realised the bear cub was an extremely valuable asset. More than just a military mascot, around Wojtek the men's morale was sky-high.

With quiet efficiency, Peter fed and cared for the young cub, who scampered after him everywhere like a young child whenever he was released from his restraining tether. Although he had his own bed, in the middle of the night the cub would often slip in beside Peter seeking warmth and comfort. Peter's comrades used to tease him and call him Mother Bear, but Peter only smiled at their jests. In fact, what they were saying was no more than the truth. In the wild, male bears have nothing to do with their offspring. Cubs are raised solely by their mothers. That Peter was Wojtek's surrogate mother was never in doubt. Whenever he was frightened or tired or in need of a cuddle, Wojtek would run to Peter and whimper until he was lifted up onto his knee. There he would sit, contentedly sucking on one of Peter's fingers.

On chilly evenings Peter would take the little bear into his army greatcoat and fasten it up so that both were protected from the cold. Cocooned inside, Wojtek would quickly fall asleep, lulled by the men's voices and the boom of Peter's laughter as they sat around their campfire swapping tales and jokes late into the night.

Remarkably quickly the little bear adapted to the company's routine. Very soon he was playing tag with the men and women in and out of the trucks. When he was a little bigger he enjoyed the rough and tumble of mock wrestling matches with anyone who would succumb to his cuddly charm. Standing upright, Wojtek would let his opponent place his hands against his front paws and try to push him backwards. This went on until the bear fell over and landed on his rump – still a feasible proposition at that early stage of his development.

When he was fully grown the wrestling matches became team events: groups of soldiers would try to rush him and knock him over. Roaring with delight, Wojtek would take on all-comers, batting them around like skittles. Occasionally, to ensure a steady stream of contestants, he would let the men win. Wrestling, of course, came naturally to Wojtek; if you have ever seen wildlife TV programmes featuring bears, you'll know the cubs are always play-fighting – a necessary part of learning new skills and developing muscle tone.

When they arrived at Wojtek's very first army base in Palestine, Wojtek set about mastering the art of tree climbing. He had a couple of false starts where his friends had to use a long ladder to fetch him out of overly high palm trees. The young cub learned that while going up palm trees was pretty much a doddle, it was married to the tiresome, but equally important, business of coming down. In his early climbing days, Wojtek simply let go and plummeted onto the ground beneath, hoping for a soft landing; as he scaled greater and greater heights this was no longer a viable option and he had to learn to descend by himself. Indeed the first time my grandfather saw Wojtek he was clinging to a tree trunk.

Wojtek's arrival in Palestine with the men meant that for the first time he experienced army life under canvas in one of the scores of static camps that were springing up all over the Middle East. As any old sweat will tell you, one dictum is true of army life: 'Hurry up and wait.' For Wojtek and his comrades, that was very much the case as General Władysł aw Anders set about overcoming the political hurdles Stalin had placed in his path to prevent the Poles re-arming and fighting as the 2nd Polish Corps alongside the British in the Western Desert. There was a protracted period when many Polish military outfits in Palestine were pretty much marking time, during which they went on plenty of training exercises and military manoeuvres; the general worked hard to trans- form his poorly equipped army, drawn from a mish-mash of disparate resources, into one of the most feared fighting forces of World War II.

My grandfather was tasked to getting these men fit for battle. For all the deprivation in the gulags, the physical wounds were superficial and could be dealt with by expert nurses and medics. Treating the mental torture was a more complicated task. The lack of nutrition had a profound effect on mind and body, but the Poles who survived the ordeal had been incredibly resilient. There is no doubt the company of the little playful animal did stimulate laughter, and although little was known then of combat stress at the time, the bear clearly play a part in the healing process in a way that no experts could have done.

# 4

## Runaway Wojtek Heads for Home

For the best part of a year Wojtek's base camp was in
Gedera, a village situated on the fringes of the Negev Desert,
in what was then Palestine. Being a military transport outfit,
the men were required to ferry supplies, and sometimes
troops, all over the Middle East. There were short runs
accomplished in a single day and also week-long journeys
that involved them staying at other camps. All was grist to
their mill. But what it meant for Wojtek was a series of
highly interesting journeys to all manner of countries including Syria, Iraq, Egypt and occasionally the Lebanon. He
loved nothing better than sitting in the cab of Peter's lorry
with its side window open, staring out at everything he
could see. He was addicted to travel and the excitement of
going to new places.

The stimulus of near-constant tourism gave him a pretty
low boredom threshold when he was back in his regular
camp and there was no one to play with. And when Wojtek
was bored, inevitably mischief followed. As a half-grown cub
he was always exploring and pushing at the boundaries of
good behaviour. Peter confided to my grandfather in a rare
moment of frankness about Wojtek's escapades that a bored
bear nearing full adulthood was a nightmare. And no
wonder. When Wojtek was fully grown and in his prime
he weighed in at some 500 pounds and, upright, stood well

over 6 feet tall. Adolescent or fully grown, Wojtek often found himself in 'jankers' on a tether, because of some mischief.

The men were remarkably tolerant of his misdeeds, even though tidying up the mayhem Wojtek would leave in his wake created a lot of additional work for them.

When not falling foul of pesky army regulations, Wojtek led the life of an officer and a gentleman. Most mornings he left Peter's tent before Reveille and went for a walk round the camp, hoping to encounter the morning's duty NCO, who usually had a biscuit or some sweetmeat for him. Then he would amble over to the cookhouse for breakfast, which included cereal, milk, bread and marmalade, biscuits and whatever else he could scrounge. Having been weaned at around six months of age, he was omnivorous, like his breed, and had a passion for fruit and honey, the latter given to him by the men and women from their own rations. After breakfast he would then head off looking for someone to play with. Being of a most amiable disposition, the Happy Warrior didn't mind whether the playmates were human or animal.

In his early days as a cub, one of his favourite pals was a large Dalmatian dog which belonged to the camp's British liaison officer. From their first meeting they were firm friends. They would tear through the camp, the bear in hot pursuit of the Dalmatian. Just as Wojtek looked like he'd catch the dog it would suddenly skid to a halt and, unable to stop himself as quickly, Wojtek would go tumbling head over heels. Neither dog nor bear cub ever tired of their boisterous game, and the outcome was always the same.

Despite having settled well into army routine, it was at Gedera that Wojtek made his one and only attempt to escape from his companions. Why he went AWOL can only be guessed. Perhaps he was bored because all of his companions were busy about their duties and he had no one to entertain him. Or perhaps he had picked up some scent that reminded him of his former mountain home – bears have an exceedingly keen sense of smell. The simplest explanation is that he was trying to escape the interminable desert heat that, in the summer months, was often so fierce it was impossible for troops to carry out military training manoeuvres. There is no doubt that Wojtek, with his thick fur, was at a distinct disadvantage when it came to keeping cool.

As a cub he had been used to the temperate climate of Hamadan province and the lower slopes of the Zagros Mountains. However, at Gedera, situated well inland and only slightly above sea level, the summer temperature ranged from 32°C to 38°C (90°F to 100°F) and in Iraq it was even higher, with the thermometer often hitting 48°C (118°F) in July and August. For Wojtek, it must have been unbearable.

In the summer at Gedera he would lie in the shadows under the water bowser, begging passing squaddies to turn on the valve. He managed to get a couple of soakings every day. When he was younger, the men dug a pit for him and filled it with water; he would lie in it long past the time it had been absorbed by the sandy earth, enjoying the coolness of the mud wallow that was left. In extremely hot weather he would remain in the mud for hours rather than face the fierce rays of the sun or hunt around for shade – which wasn't much cooler. In particularly hot weather his wallow would be filled with water twice a day.

Whatever triggered his escape bid, with typical ursine cunning Wojtek chose his moment well. It was some time before his absence from the camp was noticed. Immediately Peter and a couple of his colleagues, having ascertained from others the direction in which he was last seen heading, set off in hot pursuit. By now the runaway had put several miles of desert between him and the camp. In an inspired move, Peter commandeered the water bowser, rather than an army truck, for the chase.

When they finally caught up with him, loping towards his natal home, it was clear from his determined demeanour that he wasn't in any mood for being halted. Peter, however, released a little water from the bowser and called him by name. When the scent of the water reached him, Wojtek quickly capitulated, trading his freedom for a good soaking. Wet and cool, he was putty in Peter's hands, following the bowser the whole way back to camp in hopes of getting another drenching.

All was forgiven and Wojtek was still allowed his freedom. It was not long, however, before the mischievous bear was once again the centre of attention for all the wrong reasons, this time in a large Allied forces military camp in Iraq, to which the company was delivering supplies. In a glorious escapade reminiscent of the television series *Mash*, Wojtek went on the prowl, exploring his new quarters. His insatiable curiosity was aroused when he spotted a washing line of Polish women soldiers' underwear wafting in the breeze. Intrigued, he investigated this phenomenon and stole the lot. The half-dressed women, who had never ever encountered a very large bear in their camp, hid behind a tent, too terrified to intervene. They watched helplessly as Wojtek made off with his prizes wrapped round his head like some strange-looking washerwoman.

The women, part of a Polish signals unit, were furious because, after months of living rough in their isolated camp in the dusty desert, they had only recently taken a rare trip to Tel Aviv to acquire the much-cherished underwear. The underwear was recovered by Peter and his companions before Wojtek, in a spirit of scientific inquiry, had an opportunity to shred the women's lingerie with his sharp claws. The stolen goods were returned with some difficulty in keeping straight faces. Later they took Wojtek round to apologise – as sneaky an excuse as I've ever heard for young men to meet young women. Wojtek dutifully played his part, hiding his snout behind his large forepaws and whimpering piteously. Then he peeked out from behind his paws, his bright button eyes searching the girls' faces to see what sort of effect he was having on them. Needless to say, they were charmed. But thereafter, in camps where the Poles were sharing facilities with strangers and army outfits which didn't know the bear, a couple of soldiers were assigned the task of acting as Wojtek's minders.

However, the wily bear was still capable of giving his companions the slip when the notion took him. Again, it happened when the company was briefly stationed in Iraq on transport duty. On Christmas Eve he had participated in the Poles' traditional feast, opened his numerous presents and imbibed probably more wine than was strictly good for him. Whether it was the effects of the alcohol, no one knows, but in the wee small hours Wojtek staged his own private party. He slipped away from his sleeping companions and stealthily made his way to the camp food store. There, with considerable thoroughness, he explored the contents of everything he could open, gorging himself on jams and fruits and whatever else he could find. In his search, he ruined copious amounts of flour, grain and other comestibles, trampling them everywhere. He spilled cooking oil, tore down storage shelves and completely trashed the place. It looked as if a tornado had swept through it. Instead of enjoying their brief leisure time free of any duties, the men had to spend several hours making every-thing shipshape once more.

If it was at all possible, the men generally would conceal Wojtek's breaches of discipline and good order from the officers, reckoning what they didn't know wouldn't hurt them. Equally, the officers often turned a blind eye to many of his misdemeanours. But this particular crime was too big to ignore so Wojtek had to accept his punishment: a very firm dressing-down from Peter plus peg-and-chain confinement for the day. Fortunately for an extremely chastened Wojtek, his sentence was commuted because it was Christmas Day and he soon regained his normal freedom.

However, if his crime sheet was steadily growing, there were occasions when Wojtek redeemed himself. It was actually his obsession for water that led to his finest hour in June 1943: the day he captured an Arab spy.

As an adult bear, Wojtek would take a communal shower with the men every day in the ablutions hut. It must have looked a preposterous sight – a very large bear in the middle of naked men lathering themselves with soap while he jostled against them, trying to hog the shower heads. He had very quickly worked out that all he had to do to get a shower was to pull the string and the water would cascade over him. This he would do over and over again until stopped. Water was a precious commodity in the Allied forces' camps in the Middle East. Every drop had to be brought in by water tanker. Wojtek's usage was so profligate that eventually he had to be barred from the showers and the door locked. Undeterred, Wojtek would hang around out-side the ablutions hut like an addict, in hopes that someone using the showers would forget to lock the door or take pity on him and let him in for a water fix.

At the time the company was camped near the desert town

of Kirkuk in northern Iraq. Strategically, it was extremely important because of its huge oilfields, to which Kurds, Turks and Iraqi Arabs all laid claim. The arrival of Allied forces in this volatile, oil-rich area, already full of ethnic tensions, was not at all welcome. Out for his usual early-morning stroll around camp, Wojtek discovered to his delight that someone apparently had forgotten to relock the shower door. In a flash, the bear was inside.

Suddenly a terrified shriek pierced the air, galvanising the camp into action. Armed guards raced to the scene. There they found Wojtek cornering an Arab man in the showers. With tears running down his face, the prisoner pleaded with the guards to save him. He was marched off for interrogation where he admitted he had been spying. To escape detection after breaching the perimeter, he had picked the lock of the shower hut and crept inside, intending to sneak out again when the coast was clear to locate the camp's weapons arsenal. The Arab's spying mission was to conduct a reconnaissance for a raiding party from a nearby village the following night. However, no battle plan survives the first contact with the enemy, as he was to find out. No sooner had he crept into the ablutions hut than Wojtek was in behind him. The encounter with Wojtek so unnerved the intruder – doubtless his interrogators also threatened to renew his acquaintance with the bear – that he speedily divulged all the names of his co-conspirators. Based on his confession, the dissidents were quickly rounded up in a series of lightning raids. As for Wojtek, he was fêted like a lord and given sweetmeats and beer. As a special treat he was allowed to go for an extra-long shower at the scene of his triumph. Legend has it that it lasted so long, and consumed so much water, that afterwards a special delivery had to be organised to replenish the camp's supplies.

The 22nd Company wasn't the only Polish army outfit to have a bear as its mascot. An infantry outfit, the 16th Lwów Rifles Battalion, had been given a bear by the Shah of Persia while the men were stationed in his country. They called the bear Michael and he was several years older than Wojtek.

One day in September 1943 while Wojtek's company was stationed in Iraq he was brought to meet Wojtek. The encounter erupted into a terrifying fight. As he approached Wojtek, Michael went into a berserker rage. He wrenched his restraining chain out of the grasp of his handlers and charged at Wojtek. Within seconds the animals were grappling with each other, enveloping each other in deadly bear hugs, slashing out with terrifying claws, and each trying to rip out the other's throat with his fangs. The two titans were locked in mortal combat and there was no way the soldiers could intervene without themselves being killed or badly injured. At one point Wojtek, who was the stronger bear, began to get the better of Michael, catching him in a headlock that threatened to snap his neck. His comrades and Peter were all yelling at him to let go and, by some miracle, Wojtek finally responded to their shouts. As Wojtek pushed away his assailant Michael was separated long enough for his handlers to grab his chain and, mob-handed, get him back under control.

Michael had a completely different temperament from that of Wojtek; he had a treacherous nature and could turn vicious without warning. The officers of the 16th Lwów Rifles Battalion had attempted to rehome him with an Australian regiment, but the delinquent bear, after thumping his new handlers, made his escape and ran back to his old battalion. The men weren't keen to have him back so he was shunted onto the 22nd Company on the basis that their outfit already had experience in caring for bears. But there was no chance of Michael ever making friends with Wojtek. His hatred remained undiminished and any time he saw him he would roar out challenges and try to escape from his restraints to attack him. Thus it was, when the company later returned to Palestine, Michael was given to Tel Aviv Zoo. In thanks, its director sent the company a small monkey as a gift. The men called her Kaska.

For poor Wojtek it was a case of swapping a delinquent bear for a delinquent monkey, whose sole delight in life, right from the very first time they met, was to torment him. At every opportunity she would tweak his nose or nip his ears, jump on his head when he was asleep and race up trees to hurl stones and dates at him, chattering at him all the time. Her behaviour towards him was so bad that Wojtek would cover his eyes with his paws when he saw her coming, as if blotting her out and ignoring her would somehow save him from the nips and nastiness. The sight of Kaska chasing Wojtek through the camp was most incongruous. Indeed, it actually got to the point where the men only had to shout her name and Wojtek would turn and flee. And it wasn't just Wojtek she targeted. She would play nasty tricks on the men too, ripping up their cigarettes and thieving other items.

However, Wojtek and his companions had more to concern them than a malicious monkey. Rumours were rife that soon their company was to see action in Italy as part of the 2nd Polish Corps under General Anders. In December 1943 Wojtek and his companions were moved to Egypt, where the 2nd Corps and other British forces were mustering, preparing to sail from Alexandria and Port Said for Italy. For Peter and the men, the big question was whether the top brass would permit Wojtek to accompany them. At virtually the last minute Wojtek's special travel warrant was approved and on 13 February 1944 Wojtek and the company, aboard the converted troop ship MS Batory, set sail under protective convoy from Alexandria for the Italian port of Taranto. The Battle of Monte Cassino, in which Wojtek was to achieve legendary status, was just three months away.

# 5

# Monte Cassino: A Legend is Born

Historians still argue over whether the Battle of Monte Cassino, in which Wojtek fought with his comrades, was strategically necessary. It was the largest land battle fought in Europe in World War II, and was actually a series of four battles. The death toll was horrendously high. It is estimated it cost the lives of 60,000 men. One Polish soldier recollected: 'My battalion of 1,001 men advanced into Monte Cassino village; three days of fighting reduced it to 97 men.'

The reason for such heavy casualties was the rugged mountain terrain – and the fact that skilled German troops were making their stand at the strongest point of a powerful German defensive line known as the Gustav Line. Stretching coast-to-coast across Italy from Gaeta in the west to Ortona in the east, the Gustav Line had been prepared by the Germans long before the Allies landed in Italy. Some 10,000 men had worked for nine months constructing it along the Garigliano and Rapido rivers. It was a most formidable obstacle. Defended by 15 divisions of the German army, all seasoned troops, it had been fortified with dug-in artillery gun emplacements, concrete bunkers, machine-gun turrets, barbed wire and minefields.

The village of Monte Cassino and its nearby 1,400-year-old Benedictine monastery were regarded by the troops as the toughest section of them all on the Gustav Line. It was a virtually impregnable redoubt standing at the end of a narrow valley which the Allied troops nicknamed Death Valley. It stood between them and their next military objective, driving their way through to Rome some 80 miles away.

Unable to detour around Monte Cassino because its existence as an observation post threatened their supply lines, and already bogged down militarily for months on the beachhead it had precariously established at Anzio, the Allied advance had come to a halt in January 1944. The Germans, although heavily outnumbered, were well able to hold their positions. The mountainous terrain, ravines and rivers forced Allied tanks, military transport and guns down narrow valleys where, backed up in numerous clusters and log jams on narrow roads which were often little more than glorified tracks that could only be traversed by pack mules, they were highly vulnerable to German heavy artillery fire. Bitter weather added to the Allies' woes.

In the larger picture of the European campaign, the Battle of Monte Cassino had two other strategic goals: to facilitate break-out from the port of Anzio where the Allies had been penned in for five months and to engage as many German troops as possible in Italy so that they couldn't replenish the forces defending the coastline of France from Allied invasion.

When 2nd Polish Corps and the men of the 22nd Company arrived on the scene, three attempts to break through at Monte Cassino had already failed. The first assault took place in January and was beaten back. The second battle took place in February after heavy bombing of the monastery and its nearby village. Again the Allied troops were repulsed. A third fierce military engagement the following month was unsuccessful and left Monte Cassino in ruins.

For the fourth and final assault, named Operation Diadem, General Anders volunteered his Polish troops to spearhead the attack on the Germans' seemingly impregnable position and capture the Benedictine abbey. In the three weeks prior to that final battle, led by the Poles, it was Wojtek's company's job, along with others, to supply the artillery positions with the ordnance they needed to do the job.

It was an exceptionally hazardous business. Ammunition had to be brought to the forward positions of the forces' medium and heavy artillery so that meant 22nd Company and a number of other artillery supply companies had to drive without lights up narrow mountain roads with numerous hairpin bends. Total blackout was required for fear of alerting the enemy and drawing down a deadly artillery barrage. In complete darkness the drivers of each three-ton truck had to negotiate steep gradients, knowing that one false move could mean plunging hundreds of feet down one of the many sheer mountain precipices.

It was a slow, laborious process getting the munitions to the guns. Often the driver's mate had to walk in front of the truck, a white towel on his shoulders, guiding the vehicle. Alternatively, he would lie flat on the lorry's front mudguard, telling the driver where and when to turn. The negotiation of virtually every hairpin bend was a cumbersome and nerve-wracking business for such large vehicles which were traversing roads completely unsuitable for their size. It involved the 22nd Company drivers sawing their lorries back and forth using forward and reverse gears to get round each corner. In addition, sections of the road were enveloped by clouds of artificial fog in order to conceal any movement from German observation points; German artillery was already zeroed in on critical sections of the route.

As one Polish veteran of the campaign – 65 years on, still the proud possessor of the Wojtek insignia that was created in the bear's honour – recalls: 'When we finally pulled into the positions of our artillery, we unloaded the ammo and fuses, and after a short rest, turned around and got out as fast as possible. In spite of all our precautions, a number of trucks crashed into the steep gorges, killing their drivers.'

This, then, was the maelstrom into which Wojtek was pitchforked. It was an alien, dangerous and frightening world, and the first time he had seen action, but Wojtek very quickly adapted. Within a matter of days he went from being needy and clingy and refusing to go out in the open air because of the noise and explosions of gunfire to climbing up an exposed tree near 22nd Company's encampment and calmly observing the mysterious flashes and bangs of enemy lines being bombed, strafed and pounded by heavy artillery.

It was at this juncture that Wojtek achieved legendary status. His comrades were frantically unloading boxes of artillery shells for the Allied guns in the heat of battle. Wojtek joined them and with his paws outstretched, he indicated that he would help. Although he had never been trained to handle the unloading of 100-pound boxes of 25-pounder shells, shell fuses and other supplies, he simply observed what the men were doing and joined in, without any bidding. Standing upright, he held out his front paws into which men loaded the heavy boxes of shells. Effortlessly, he carried the munitions to their storage areas beside the artillery positions, and returned to the lorries to collect more. It was the company's proud boast that he never dropped a single shell. However, it has to be said he did the lifting very much on his own terms: he chose when and how long he would work. At times he had to be wheedled into helping out. If he decided to stop and lie down for a bit, a titbit or two at either end of his supplies run could reinvigorate his war effort. In actual fact, during the Battle of Monte Cassino, Wojtek's company supplied approximately 17,300 tons of ammunition, 1,200 tons of fuel and 1,100 tons of food for Polish and British troops.

On 11 May 1944, the final battle of Monte Cassino began. Before the attack General Anders addressed his troops, telling them: 'For this action let the lion's spirit enter your hearts and keep deep in your heart God, honour and our land – Poland.' He urged his men to go and take a revenge for all the suffering in Poland, for what they, themselves, had suffered in the many years spent in Russia and for the years of separation they had endured from their families.

At 11 p.m. – H-hour – some 1,200 Allied guns opened up. Their coordinated artillery fire was so great that it practically turned night into bright day. It was a shock-and-awe engagement where the very ground shook. But Wojtek stayed with his comrades, ensuring the munitions got through.

All along the Gustav Line, Allied troops were engaging the enemy in attacks which resulted in the wholesale slaughter of their men. The single most critical phase of the battle was the crossing of the Rapido River under the German guns. If that failed so did the offensive.

At separate points, infantrymen of numerous nationalities attempted the crossing, including the 8th Indian Division far west of Monte Cassino at San Angelo and the 4th British Division just west of the town near the railway cuttings. The 2nd Polish Corps' task was to cross the river and advance up the north-east flank of the monastery at Hill 593.

That most decisive phase of the battle to capture Monte Cassino was recalled by Black Watch veteran John Clarke MBE. He recalled that the river crossings attempted by the Poles and their British counterparts were almost a complete disaster: 'To cross the river, canvas folding boats had been sent from Burma. They had only arrived a few hours before zero hour. Attacking infantrymen assembled the boats and set off across the swift-flowing river. Many were simply swept away to their deaths.'

Other men drowned within yards of setting out. Their boats sank almost instantly because the canvas sides were riddled with holes caused by insects which had infested them during their storage in the Far East. The men in the canvas boats were mostly soldiers from the Argylls and the Hampshires, although the attrition rates were so high that many others, including Poles, were brought in as re-inforcements. And all this was happening before the Germans, from their well-protected positions, laid down withering curtains of artillery fire.

Against all the odds, some of the troops made it to the other side and established several frail bridgeheads. As they dug in amid the smoke and the river mist they faced a new and unexpected danger. The soil around them was heavily impregnated with phosphorus. They disturbed it as they dug their foxholes and there arose an eerie glow which made the troops easy targets for German snipers.

Every yard the troops advanced was bought with the blood of brave men. The carnage was almost beyond computation. Nowhere was the fighting more brutal than on the route being forced to the top by the 2nd Polish Corps. For six days and nights the battle raged. With fanatical courage the Poles hurled themselves at the entrenched positions of the Germans on the hill leading up to the monastery; it was as if a great and implacable hatred for all the agonies visited on their country by German invaders was driving them to feats of superhuman endurance. At one point, cut off from their supplies, Polish troops who had run out of ammunition resorted to throwing stones at the enemy.

Tomasz Skrzynski, then a 20-year-old cadet in the Carpathian Lancers Regiment, who would later be part of 22nd Company with Wojtek, was with the Poles in the uplands above the monastery. Like other Polish soldiers, he had been fighting at close quarters to gain control of the hilltop. But when the savagery of hand-to-hand combat was over, there was no respite. He and his comrades were forced to spend days sheltering in crude foxholes and a ruined stone hut to escape enemy shelling. When they dug into the ground there they uncovered the corpses of three Germans, whom they reburied, marking their grave with a makeshift cross.

'The shelling continued day and night, and there was no such thing as silence,' he recalled many decades later, in an interview with the BBC. 'At one point I was ordered to count the shells falling nearby, but after two hours or so it was above 500 and I lost count.' The months of battle and constant shelling had turned the normally lush countryside into a wasteland. 'There was no greenery, only stumps of trees. Everywhere just stumps, as far as you could see,' said Skrzynski.

The battle raged on until the Poles prevailed. They finally walked into the ruins of the monastery on 18 May 1944 without a shot being fired, having spotted a tattered white flag of surrender. Inside they discovered a number of Germans in ragged uniforms, three badly wounded paratroopers and numerous corpses. As the Poles raised a Lancers Regiment pennant to signify the capture of the monastery, a soldier played an ancient bugle call recognised by all Poles. Known as the Kraków Hejnał, according to legend it was used to alert that city to an invasion by Genghis Khan's Mongol hordes. As the notes rang out, the Polish troops wept with exhaustion and relief that the fighting had ended. The carnage was over. In the week's fighting 2nd Corps suffered appalling losses. There were a total of 4,199 casualties, including 1,150 killed. It was one of the decisive battles of the war.

Elsewhere along the Gustav Line, other victories were achieved. With his mates from the 6th Black Watch, John Clarke crossed the Rapido on a bridge constructed by the

Royal Engineers to take the weight of tanks. The bridge was built while the sappers came under constant enemy fire – an incredible feat. Clarke recalls: 'They performed miracles erecting that bridge, but their losses were terrible. I crossed with the Black Watch. All around were bodies and craters where shells had landed. We formed up, fixed bayonets and moved on. Then a really thick mist came down and our CO, Colonel Madden, lined up the tanks of the Lothian and Border Horse and placed the lads around the tanks. Then we moved on through the mist. We fought for five days and nights before reaching our target of Highway Six. This meant the German paras were cut off.'

In a separate engagement, Algerian, Moroccan and Tunisian troops of the French Expeditionary Corps achieved another extremely important breakthrough in the Aurunci Mountains south of the Liri River. The combined victories forced the enemy to retreat.

On the morning of 18 May 1944, Private Clarke and his Black Watch comrades were withdrawn from the battle in trucks and taken to Monte Cassino, then in the hands of the Poles. Clarke said: 'When it was all over and we rested in Cassino town, we had a brew and a preliminary roll-call. We sat among the ruins of the old cathedral when a tubby, red-faced individual came bouncing up to us. He had a tape recorder in a wooden box hanging from his neck and said: "Hello, lads, I'm Wynford Vaughan-Thomas from the BBC. Nothing to worry about now – you're out of it."

'I'll never forget what happened next. Not a word was said by our lads. Eyes turned towards this horrible creature and locked onto his face. The silence and the stares lasted several minutes until, completely unnerved by it, the man turned and ran away in embarrassment.'

What Vaughan-Thomas, one of the BBC's most celebrated

war correspondents, did not know was that in the roll-call just taken the men of the Black Watch had learned that they had suffered 60 per cent casualties.

John Clarke is now aged 86 and lives in Manchester. Still honorary secretary of the Monte Cassino Veterans Association, he said: 'It was then that we all made a promise never to forget those lads we were leaving behind. We have kept that promise. About this time a flag of some kind was raised in the ruins of the monastery. It was raised by the Poles. Just as we were leaving Cassino another flag was raised. It was the Union Jack.'

Wojtek's actions during the Battle of Monte Cassino were to give rise to the proudest and most sought-after piece of military regalia in 22nd Company: a special badge featuring Wojtek going to war. Based on a drawing by one of the soldiers, it depicted him carrying an artillery shell and also featured a truck steering wheel to indicate that he was part of a transport company. The Poles wore it either as a cap badge or on the sleeves or lapels of their combat tunics. It was very much 22nd Company's trademark: the bear logo even appeared on regimental equipment. Within weeks of it being created and approved, shortly after the Battle of Monte Cassino, the Wojtek military logo was everywhere. The bear had pretty much become a legend in his own not inconsiderable lunchtime as curious Allied soldiers from other regiments inquired about the badge's significance.

Wojtek had been well and truly blooded in one of the most controversial and historic engagements of World War II. Perhaps the most amazing aspect of it was that being exposed to the rigours of intensive warfare didn't alter his temperament at all.

Some readers may suspect that Wojtek's shell-carrying exploits have gained a little in the telling, but soldiers from other regiments witnessed the bear in action. In April 1944, in the build-up to the final battle, Black Watch veteran John Clarke and a friend, Vincent Franchetti, were foraging for food near the village of Acquafondata, some six miles from Monte Cassino. Their battalion had just been taken out of the front line and the men were making the most of the lull in the fighting. They had enjoyed a much-needed shower at the village and set off, as Clarke says, 'on the scrounge', into the heavily wooded countryside.

Clarke testifies: 'I remember it clearly because it was my twentieth birthday. We were making our way through the deserted fields, looking for stray hens and eggs, when a nearby artillery unit opened fire. We went to look and found a battery of Polish gunners setting up for a barrage. The gun site was hidden in a clearing within a large wood. As we watched, suddenly out of the wood came a large bear, walking on its hind legs. It seemed to be carrying something. Both Vincent and I shouted a warning to the gunners that a bear was going towards them, but nobody responded.

'The bear went up to the trail legs of the artillery gun and placed a shell on the ground. The bear then went back into the wood and reappeared with another shell. By this time, we had realised that the bear was tame and most likely a circus bear. We just went on our way.'

There was to be an interesting postscript to Clarke's memory of the encounter. After the war, when he told his wife the story, she refused to believe it, dismissing it as a tall tale he had invented. She would often persuade him to recount it to friends, still scoffing about its accuracy. However, the tables were turned when the couple were at a function attended by Polish veterans. Once more Clarke was persuaded to recite his tale. 'Ah yes,' said one of the Poles. 'That would be Wojtek.'

Later on, on a memorial trip to Kraków, Clarke actually met Tomasz Skrzynski, who had been involved in looking after Wojtek and who was wearing the famed bear logo on his jacket lapel. Clarke says he claimed that he had helped train the bear.

There is proof, too, from another quarter that Wojtek was used to toting burdens for his friends. One of the Polish DPs in Scotland after the war, Augustyn Karolewski, who died in 2012, and a retired river-salmon fisherman, recalled Wojtek's behaviour at Sunwick Farm. At that time Karolewski, known as Kay to the Scots (a nickname which derived from the fact that the only word of English he knew when he first arrived at Winfield Camp was 'OK'), was living at Winfield Camp while employed locally as a farm labourer. Wojtek often accompanied the men to the fields where they were working and was quite happy to carry fencing staves and logs for them, although it has to be said the bear was usually more interested in attempting to steal the contents of the men's lunch tins. Nevertheless, it is proof of a sort that Wojtek was well used to carrying heavy loads for his friends. The simple dynamic at work was comradeship.

Monte Cassino was a turning point in the fortunes of the Allies. The months of May and June saw many successes. May saw American forces break out of Anzio after five long months, forcing a German retreat. June saw the fall of Rome to the Allies – and the long-awaited D-Day invasion. Following the Battle of Monte Cassino, 2nd Corps took part in the drive up the Adriatic coast, capturing the Italian port of Ancona on 20 July 1944 supported by 22nd Company. It was an important victory because it gave the Allies access to a port which greatly shortened their supply lines as they drove their way northwards up the spine of Italy.

For the men of 22nd Company there was little respite. As

the exigencies of war dictated, their billets were constantly changing, ranging from military camps to farm dwellings in the countryside. It was during such a period when they were stationed at a farm that Wojtek rediscovered his primal hunting instincts – and for the first time challenged his mentor Peter's authority in a terrifying display of rage.

The men had noticed many times that around horses, and particularly donkeys, Wojtek's whole demeanour would change: spotting them grazing in a field he would drop onto all fours and would start stalking them. Usually a shout from his mentor, Peter, or one of the soldiers who knew the bear, was sufficient to deflect him from his purpose. But on one occasion he set about stalking a donkey with serious intent to kill. The terrified animal broke free from its tether and tried to escape. It was only the intervention of Peter which prevented bloodshed. As Wojtek loped after the donkey, Peter jumped onto his back and covered the bear's eyes with his hands, a method he sometimes employed when Wojtek became overly excitable. But this time the tactic to break the bear's focus didn't work. Wojtek reared up on his hind legs and Peter was forced to dismount and employ even more desperate measures. Running round to stand in front of Wojtek, he blocked his progress and roared at him to stop. For one heart-stopping moment, Wojtek reared to his full height and bared his fangs at his mentor, prepared to destroy him. Then he remembered who Peter was and immediately became submissive.

It was a confrontation which didn't dent Peter's calm faith in Wojtek, but he knew it was no longer possible for him to be constantly on hand to control the bear. If other minders weren't available, Wojtek would have to be tethered more frequently. The need for a restraint was underlined on another occasion when the company was quartered near Loreto, where Wojtek stalked and cornered a pack horse in a field. However, this time the bear had met his match. Crazed with fear, the horse lashed out with its hooves and gave Wojtek a heavy blow to the head. Dazed and disconcerted, Wojtek ran off. His hunting days were apparently over.

For the rest of that year, and into the following spring, as the Allied advance continued to press the Germans into retreat, 22nd Company was as busy as ever, but there were lighter moments. On one occasion, while 22nd Company was in transit and taking a short break in a field, Wojtek snuck off along the road and went exploring. At a crossroads, he discovered a mobile crane parked at the roadside and climbed up its tower to stage an impromptu acrobatic performance that brought military traffic in all directions to a complete standstill. There was an almighty snarl-up which stretched back for the best part of a mile in every direction while Wojtek performed his aerial tricks high above the ground. Never happier than when he was the centre of attention, he refused to come down until a bottle of beer was produced to tempt him back to earth.

In another legendary incident he almost got himself shot. At night, in camp, if Peter wasn't around, Wojtek would often slip into his mates' tents and bed down beside them; he'd been doing it since he was a cub and the men were quite used to it. He liked the companionship as well as the warmth of body contact. However, on this occasion the company was sharing a camp with numerous other Allied soldiers who had no knowledge of Wojtek's nocturnal habits. The bear strayed off his section into another unit's camp and invaded the tent of a group of Indian soldiers who were greatly disconcerted at the appearance of a huge bear in their midst. Still in their nightclothes, the panic-stricken men grabbed their rifles and levelled them at Wojtek, ready to shoot him if he made any move towards them. Alerted by the commotion, the camp guards dashed to the scene. By good fortune they happened to be Polish and knew the bear, so they were able to defuse the situation without a tragedy occurring. But it had been a close-run thing.

The last battle fought by 2nd Corps on Italian soil was in April 1945, when the Poles captured Bologna from the Germans. Again, 22nd Company was in the thick of it. The following month the war in Europe ended with Germany's surrender.

The end of the war was to herald in an idyllic summer for Wojtek and his companions. There were plenty of furloughs and he had many opportunities to indulge his passion for water sports; he enjoyed many happy days swimming in the temperate waters of the Adriatic. As ever, his mischievous nature was given full rein. The beaches where he and the men bathed were shared with civilians. Wojtek's favourite trick was to swim underwater towards a group of unsuspecting women bathers, then suddenly surface in their midst. Their squeals of alarm as they found themselves in close proximity to a huge bear were music to his ears. To Wojtek it was a great joke and he never tired of it. Perhaps you could say he was the furry Jaws of his time, long before cinemagoers were scared witless by the creepy music that indicated the arrival of the giant shark. It was also an excellent way for the Polish soldiers to meet young women: Wojtek would ignore the men's shouts for him to come back, preferring to romp around in the water near his victims, so the soldiers would have to swim out and fetch him. There is no record of whether this unusual dating technique ever brought about the desired results for the soldiers.

Wojtek was often genuinely reluctant to abandon his new-found female friends when it was time to return to camp.

When he refused to leave the water, his companions had one
sure-fire method of getting him back on dry land. One of the
soldiers would wade ashore and leap into the military truck
and start it up, as if to drive off. At the sound of the engine
Wojtek's ears would prick up and he would immediately stop
what he was doing and come tearing out of the water. He had
a tremendous fear of being left behind and the truck trick
worked like a charm every time.

Indeed, on many of their trips inland Wojtek preferred to
sit alone in the cab, awaiting the men's return from whatever
duties they were carrying out, just as he had done in the
Middle East. Given the immense shortages of goods in both
theatres of war, it was not surprising that petty theft was rife,
indeed raised almost to a national art form, so Wojtek's
presence acted as a formidable deterrent. Nothing was ever
stolen from Wojtek's truck when he was in residence.

While 22nd Company was kept busy loading and unloading goods at docks along the coast, there was a more leisurely
pace to life and everyone made the most of it. In September
1946 they finally set sail for Glasgow from Naples. This time
Private Wojtek was officially listed on the passenger manifest.
As on his first sea crossing, from Egypt to Italy, Wojtek once
again found himself the centre of attention and his wrestling
matches with his companions were very much the highlight
of the voyage. That was the lighter side of military life, and a
much-needed distraction. In truth, the men and Wojtek had
no idea of what lay ahead for them in Scotland, a country
about which they knew virtually nothing.

# 6

# Rationing . . . and a Bear Who Needs 300 Apples a Day

When Wojtek proudly marched through Glasgow with the veterans of 22nd Company, Polish Army Service Corps (Artillery), to the cheers of the crowds lining the streets, it must have seemed to the Polish troops that September 1946 was a special month. For the first time they felt they were genuinely entering a period of new beginnings. While it was gratifying to be hailed by Glasgow citizens as the heroes of Monte Cassino – which they indubitably were – they were more interested in winning the peace than winning the battle.

It was a time when the future stretching out in front of the newcomers seemed filled with both optimism and hope: optimism that they would soon be reunited with their loved ones; hope that they would be able to pick up the threads of their disrupted lives and create a new and secure future for themselves and their families.

They arrived in Scotland the same month that the UK set up the Polish Resettlement Corps (PRC), a non-combatant unit of the British army. Its initial purpose was to help Polish troops to retrain for civilian life in Britain. Over a maximum period of two years, those who became members of the PRC were to be housed in camps across the UK. There they would learn English and a trade before being permitted to seek employment. The PRC was also to be used as a clearing house to help repatriate the Poles. The men of 2nd Corps –

including 22nd Company – were the very first troops to be encouraged to participate in the new resettlement programme, and many of those stationed at Winfield Camp did.

The men of 2nd Corps were pulled out of Italy and transported to Britain to accommodate the demands of Stalin. The Soviets had no wish to have a standing army of some 250,000 Poles in mainland Europe, most of whom had a deep hatred of Communist Russia for all the cruelties it had inflicted on their nation. Polish troops in the West were still serving under British operational command, but even so, 2nd Corps' presence in Italy represented a destabilising influence in the mind of the ever-suspicious Stalin. He had no wish to see them return to their homeland.

Following the conference of the major powers at Potsdam in 1945, on the basis of his bare-faced lie that he later would permit free Polish elections, Stalin gained control of Poland. But it was really *fait accompli* even before the conference. He wanted nothing to threaten that arrangement.

When the conference set the country's new postwar boundaries, Poland was required to cede part of its territory to Russia while gaining a section of Germany. But that was a mere fig leaf. The British government was forced to de-recognize Poland's government-in-exile, based in London, saying its members would have to return to Poland to participate in the new elections when they came. However, Stalin had already established an interim government, known as the Polish Committee of National Liberation, that was a vassal of the Soviet Union. As his iron grip on the country tightened, the process of weeding out 'undesirables' and installing placemen to run the oppressive state apparatus was already well under way.

Marching along the Broomielaw in Glasgow, the men of 22nd Company had little or no knowledge of these political machinations. They also knew very little of what had actually happened to their country during the later stages of the war – except that it was very bad. Nevertheless, as they arrived in Scotland, morale was high.

In part, that was due to the lengthy period of rest and recuperation they had had in Italy. On the sunny Adriatic coast, since the war's end, the company had enjoyed the warm climate and an abundance of soft fruits and vegetables. Alas, a rude shock awaited both men and bear after they disembarked from their troop ship in Glasgow. There was to be no easy transition into a civilian existence and they also found themselves domiciled in an austere Scotland where food rationing was a way of life.

In Scotland the food allowance each person had to get by on at that time included the following: 2 ounces of bacon or ham, a finger of cheese (1.5 ounces), 7 ounces of butter or margarine, 2 ounces of cooking fats, 8 ounces of sugar, 2 ounces of tea (about 20 teabags), 4 ounces of sweets and 1 shilling's-worth (5p) of meat. It doesn't sound too bad, does it? Except this wasn't a day's ration – it was for one full week. Except for the bacon. That was two weeks' allowance. Other staples such as bread, bananas and even potatoes (throughout 1947) were also rationed. As for fresh eggs, you could have one a fortnight – if you could lay your hands on one. Most urban families made do with the vile-tasting powdered version for the skimpy amounts of baking they could eke out of their precious rations of flour and sugar. On the plus side, people were allowed three pints of milk a week.

In fact, milk was just about the only commodity with which the Attlee government was generous; as part of its drive to maintain the nutritional health of the country's children, in 1946 free school milk was introduced for all pupils up to the age of 18. This was later reduced to primary schools only. A quarter of a century later, free school milk was finally phased out by Margaret Thatcher. She was dubbed Thatcher the Milk Snatcher by her political opponents.

Those of us of a certain age well remember the crates of one-third-of-a-pint bottles which had to be humped in from the playground into the classrooms. For some unfathomable reason, once indoors, the crates always seemed to be stacked next to the school radiators, ensuring the milk was lukewarm by the time it was dispensed. It is one of life's ironies that, despite food shortages and rationing, the children of postwar Scotland were better fed than many of their modern counterparts. That, in large part, was down to the free milk ration and free school meals (about half the UK's pupils qualified for them), plus daily doses of free cod liver oil and concentrated orange juice which mothers determinedly rammed down the throats of protesting offspring.

However, Wojtek, when it came to rations in austerity Scotland, broke the mould. Clearance for his registration as a private in the Polish army had come through on St Valentine's Day, 1945. As he was now formally on the books, the company could indent for provisions for him. But as he required an intake of around 20,000 calories a day – the equivalent of around 300 apples or, say, 60 hamburgers – keeping him well fed was quite a challenge.

Like his brown-bear brothers in Iran, Wojtek always beefed up considerably in the autumn, putting on as much as 1.5 pounds in weight per day if the feeding was particularly good, as it had been in Italy. Most bears, whether they hibernate or not (and Wojtek didn't), spend up to 16 hours a day – virtually all their waking hours – foraging.

In passing, hibernation isn't all it's cracked up to be – many breeds of bear burn up almost the same energy when asleep as they do awake. Their metabolic rate doesn't drop significantly. If Wojtek had been back in the Zagros Mountains he probably would have hibernated, or perhaps more accurately, remained semi-dormant in his lair. However, he didn't because he was being fed on a daily basis, and, probably more significantly, his comrades didn't hibernate. In virtually all respects, Wojtek considered himself no different from human beings.

Fortunately for 22nd Company, Wojtek wasn't fussy about what he ate, as long as there was plenty of it. Like his breed, he was omnivorous; he would eat almost any type of food including carrion, fish, birds, meat, grasses, fruit, root vegetables, fibrous roots, wild berries, broad-leaved plants and shrubs, tree leaves, and, when he could get them, grubs, ants and honey. In the ground, on the ground or above the ground, it really didn't matter: Wojtek was up for eating it, although his first port of call was always the camp cookhouse.

About 80 per cent of his diet was vegetarian. In their transit camp, before they moved to the Borders, it cannot always have been easy for the soldiers to ensure their comrade was getting the 40 to 80 pounds of vegetable fodder he required daily. When the company moved to its new home, Winfield Camp, it still remained a considerable challenge for them until country folk started dropping in at the camp with scraps for the bear. As for Wojtek, he quickly adapted to Borders life, foraging for leaves and plants until there was hardly any greenery left on the trees and bushes in the immediate vicinity of the camp.

Although a very clean bear, his eating habits were quite childlike. First he would pick out the items of food he really liked, leaving to last the less interesting fodder. Although far away from his native nectarines, apricots and other exotic fruits, his diet was as good as any in the district. He received many gifts of food from visitors. He had a keen nose for any crumbs which might be lingering in a pocket or a handbag, so there were often raids on unsuspecting visitors' clothing and property. Though he received severe reprimands for his attempted thefts, the temptation was always there and he would nearly always succumb to it.

At the camp, special sleeping quarters for Wojtek were built: a small wooden hut which the men speedily knocked up for him and lined with straw. From his new home there was much for the bear to see. The prickly Scottish blackthorn hedges nearby were a new phenomenon for Wojtek, and he soon learned they offered considerable entertainment from the wildlife which inhabited them. He would stare at the hedges for hours, watching birds hop around inside them. Occasionally rabbits and hares passed through, as did the odd fox. From time to time sheep would become entangled in them and cattle would come along to eat the long grasses beside the hedge boundaries. Since his hut was situated between two hedges he had a great view of the local wildlife. For an easily bored bear this must have been the equivalent of watching TV.

Wojtek was especially good at being still if he had to be. He would flatten himself on the ground, watching and listening. When the sparrows became too cocky, too noisy and, most crucially, too close, suddenly a furry apparition would rise up and pounce, with little thought of the consequences other than satisfying a deep call from the wild. The process would be repeated many times, much to the detriment of the hedges. Eventually they died a slow but natural death because of his depredations and fences had to be erected. The wildlife show was over. However, new forms of entertainment were eventually found and, besides, there were always the hedges on the other side of the road.

Long before the hedges vanished, Wojtek had his own scouting methods down pat. Perched up a tree, he would scan the camp entrance for any interesting developments. From his vantage point, Wojtek had an uncanny knack of identifying visitors who were arriving at Winfield Camp with food. Actually, it was not his sight, which like that of all bears was poor, but his acute sense of smell which resulted in him making a swift descent from his tree to swoop upon the newcomer.

For those who knew Wojtek, the enthusiastic welcome they received was not unexpected. He would rear to his full height, wave his paws about and perform a quick roll of submission on the ground before bounding towards them. Often the locals were bringing commodities like jam, eggs and honey to the camp, but Wojtek knew there was always a treat set aside for him. He very quickly came to recognise the faces of those regularly bringing food to the camp as opposed to visitors calling in for a chat. From the latter he could expect, at best, a cigarette or the occasional boiled sweet. These treats were welcome, but not in the same league as the goodies provided by the other callers. A hard-boiled egg was of particular interest once opened – the shell was consumed as well.

Despite his awe-inspiring stature, Wojtek was a gentle giant. He liked to touch and be touched, a wondrously strange thing for a beast which, in the wild, was both solitary and dangerous. He had a fascination for people's eyes and ears and, for those brave enough to let him, he liked to touch their faces. He had a delicacy of touch which was surprising in such a large beast. With a sharp, six-inch claw he could push a tiny black beetle along the ground without hurting it, playing and toying with it for ages until either he got bored with his game or the insect discovered a bolthole and escaped.

Wojtek also liked to be groomed, especially around the back of his head and ears, which he found difficult to reach without aid of a stick. For an urgent itch, a tree or a fence would do the trick and he would vigorously rub himself against these scratching posts until it subsided. It wasn't too long before the trees around Sunwick Farm bore the permanent scars of his activities, their bark ripped and scored by his claws through a mixture of climbing and scratching. Quite a few were killed off. No one ever complained.

It was on Monday, 28 October 1946, that Wojtek and his companions first arrived at Winfield Camp and, as seasoned campaigners of such moves, rapidly settled in – Wojtek to his special hut and his comrades to their Nissen huts.

It was hardly gracious living. The men slept 30 to a hut, dormitory-style, in beds arranged against the walls of their barracks. With roofs and walls of corrugated iron, cold concrete floors and thin-paned, small, draughty windows, Nissen huts were poorly insulated. Each hut was heated by a wood- and coal-burning pipe stove. Situated, as these were, either in the centre or at one end of the hut, the stoves had to be stoked until they were red-hot if they were to keep out the penetrating night chill. Even then the heat barely reached a few feet down the length of the hut before it evaporated. In winter, the huts were freezing.

The winter of 1946–47 was one of the harshest on record, with temperatures plummeting to well below freezing. In parts of the country snow drifts reached heights of 23 feet and even the English Channel occasionally became impassable because of pack ice as the temperature dropped to $-23°C$. The intense cold led to the authorities' allocating extra coal to Winfield Camp, but the combination of the low temperatures outside and the frost gathering inside the corrugated-iron interior roof meant the warmer the hut became, the more the frost melted and dripped onto the beds below. This was a source of hilarity among the men at first, but long nights of dripping water and constant dampness were really no laughing matter. After many sleepless nights tempers became frayed as they sought vainly to get some rest. Their conditions were miserable. The only relief came when the drips refroze to become small icicles dotted all along the curved sides of their inadequate shelters. The huts' wooden doors posed another problem. Made from poorly cured wood, the constant damp caused them to swell, making them stick every time they were opened and closed.

Wojtek, however, had no such problems curling up in his straw and doing what bears do best – sleep. With a fur coat to rival anything from the purveyors of fine pelts, he had a definite advantage over his comrades when it came to bedding down in any situation.

On the plus side, the extreme weather created new work opportunities for the Poles, who were needed for road clearing and assisting locals with the delivery of food supplies and coal; the weather crisis added new purpose to their lives. It comes as no surprise that these fit young men enjoyed showing off their prowess in wielding shovels and brushes alongside their Scottish neighbours. The whole community came out to help, but the Poles enjoyed their role as snow heroes and often posed for the occasional photograph.

It has to be remembered that home comforts weren't much different for the local populace. Central heating and double glazing were decades away from everyday use. Apart from special occasions when the parlour fire was lit, most people's homes had only a single room that was heated – usually the kitchen. Stepping out of the warmth of the kitchen onto the hallway linoleum was like stepping out onto ice. Bedrooms were like iceboxes too. As a girl I regularly got up in the morning to find the windows completely opaque with the delicate traceries of heavy frost. To be honest, in the Borders we thought nothing of it. For men who had recently experienced searing desert heat followed by the more comfortable warmth of a Mediterranean climate, it must have taken a bit of getting used to.

Still, it was autumn when Wojtek and the men of 22nd Company arrived at Winfield Camp and as yet the rigours of a Borders winter, and all that it entailed, were a few months off. Wojtek liked his new habitat and was quick to explore its environs, tasting and eating new types of vegetation that he hadn't previously encountered. He was completely invigorated by the change of locale and energetically joined in the men's tasks, such as collecting and breaking firewood for the cookhouse. There are no prizes for guessing the wages he demanded for his labours.

The 22nd Company shared Winfield Camp with other detachments of Poles who had never met Wojtek. Mindful of the incident in Italy when the bear had almost got himself shot by straying into a tent full of strangers in the middle of the night, Peter Prendys took the precaution of chaining him up when he wasn't around. Wojtek was now always chained up overnight and occasionally during the day when there was no one to keep an eye on him. When his regular minders were around, however, he still had the run of the camp, and would go strolling round the Nissen huts to greet his friends.

Not unnaturally, Wojtek was a big attraction to local children, who would often come up to the camp to see the huge, exotic animal. For them the excitement was simply to get close, to stroke his fur or to give him a titbit, which he always accepted most politely. However, one day a local boy decided to play a prank on Wojtek, by wrapping a sweet paper round a stone and giving it to him. Wojtek, who had a very sweet tooth, swiftly unwrapped his present using his highly mobile and dexterous lips. When he discovered he had been tricked he let out an angry roar and with lightning speed grabbed his tormentor. The squeals of the captive boy and Wojtek's roaring quickly brought Polish soldiers running to investigate the commotion and Wojtek released the boy. Order having been restored, they questioned the lad about what had happened. Shamefaced, the boy confessed, and it was he, not Wojtek, who got the telling-off.

While Wojtek was eternally fascinating to children (and he liked them too), adults weren't immune to his charms and often would stop by. One of the most regular visitors was my grandfather, Jim Little. He called in several times a week to check that the men in the camp had everything they needed, and no trip was complete without a social call on Wojtek. Bear and man would stand there of an evening, communing sociably, Jim chain-smoking as usual. Every so often the bear would hold out a huge paw, asking for a cigarette and would usually be given one, which he ate with great gusto. Oddly enough, the cigarette always had to be lit. If it wasn't he would throw it away. He only ate lit cigarettes. Perhaps there was an aroma of burning tobacco that he liked, or perhaps they had to be exactly the same as the cigarettes the men had in their mouths; no one has ever solved the mystery. He never appeared to burn himself as he chomped on them.

It was a strange friendship between my grandfather and the bear. They may have shared the same small vice of cigarettes but there their paths diverged. My grandfather was a staunch teetotaller while Wojtek would have sold his soul to the devil for a bottle of beer. He had a huge liking for alcohol and obviously enjoyed its effect. He was rationed to two bottles of beer a day when it was available. But on high days and holidays, when he talked his way into a bottle of wine, he occasionally got tipsy and would go about the camp, as they say in Scotland, 'by the light of his eye'. A Happy Warrior, indeed.

On occasion, Wojtek's bear side outweighed his human traits. When it came to food he was an incorrigible sneak thief, always with an eye out for the main chance. One bleak autumn day, with a bitter wind blowing in off the North Sea which was visible from the camp, Wojtek was on the prowl. Coming from the cookhouse was the magnificent smell of freshly prepared food. The scent was irresistible for a hungry bear. Everyone was aware of Wojtek's weakness for food so around the cookhouse strict security was always observed. The doors into the kitchens were always firmly closed because Wojtek's fellow soldiers knew that if he spotted a chink in the cookhouse defences there was absolutely no way of stopping him if he decided to make a lightning raid. When a 500-pound bear is on the make, and hellbent on going through an incautiously open door to reach food, you just have to get out of his way.

This particular day there were no doors open, and un-suspecting kitchen staff, many of them local girls who arrived daily to prepare meals for the camp, were going about their usual chores. Wojtek, when he was casing the joint, had noted the kitchen windows were open to release the steam and heat from the boiling pots and pans in the kitchen. The scent of the cooking was irresistible. With a great deal of misplaced optimism, he crept up to one of the Nissen hut windows and started to climb through it.

Peter Prendys, hearing first screams of alarm, then howls of laughter, knew instantly that the bear was involved. He dashed to the cookhouse as Polish servicemen began appear-ing from all directions. There they found Wojtek firmly stuck in the metal-framed window, half in, half out.

Head in the kitchens, body outside, he was struggling frantically to escape. With the smell of food still in his nostrils, he was still bent on getting inside – a task that was becoming even more difficult because a group of soldiers were clinging to his body and hind legs and were pulling him in the other direction. Watching this bizarre tug-of-war, the local workers trapped inside the hut didn't know whether to laugh or scream. After some considerable time, Wojtek was extracted from the window and given a thorough dressing-down by Peter for his bad manners and disgraceful behaviour.

No one could chastise Wojtek like Peter. When on the receiving end of one of Peter's scoldings, the bear had a well-practised penitent's routine. First he would pretend to cry, covering his eyes with his huge front paws. Then, after a decent interval, he would peep through them to check Peter's reaction. If the response was good, without being told, he would go into submissive mode and lie on his back as a sign he was sorry. But if Peter was still angry, Wojtek would stay in his childlike 'crying' position until Peter stalked off, or until forgiveness had been made clear.

The cookhouse window incident proved to be a one-off. Later, when passing the building, Wojtek would sniff wistfully but confine his activities to loitering hopefully at the door. Occasionally his sense of mischief would get the better of him – and he would give the door a quick push if it was ajar, and then beat a hasty retreat. He was no doubt testing the water to see if anyone reacted; there was also a chance that by announcing his presence scraps might be forthcoming. But he had learned that a certain level of behaviour was required – namely, that he stay outside.

The camp servicemen had to be careful with discarded tins, especially those with jagged edges which could have injured him; Wojtek was always on the lookout for new food sources.

No receptacle was left unexamined. Whether placed in rubbish bins or buried in the ground, it would take only a moment for him to unearth a tin and extract the most meagre morsel of discarded food with his long claws. Thus nothing was left to chance. Tins were flattened and bottles emptied of their contents. The men knew the keen Wojtek nose was part radar, part windsock; if there was a food source to be found he quickly homed in on its scent. But his ability to unearth hidden scraps of food was not always unerring. Often it depended on which way the wind was blowing; if he was upwind of a cache of forbidden tins he didn't pick up its smell.

Wojtek's keen powers of observation alerted him to upcoming entertainments at the camp. He very quickly realised that the preparation of large pots of coffee indicated that a gathering of sorts, either for singing or dancing, was in the offing. Another giveaway was the sudden surge of activity in the ablutions hut as the men prepared themselves for the evening ahead with their limited grooming aids. Carbolic soap, Brylcreem and a decent comb were about as good as it got, but there were the occasional gifts of scented soaps or lavender water (in lieu of aftershave) which added to the sense of occasion. The men took great care with their appearance. In fact, it was not unusual for them to paint their fingernails with clear varnish. That may sound somewhat effeminate, but that was far from being the case. They were as tough as (varnished) nails.

Preparing for a dance when Wojtek was around was sometimes difficult. To the bear, the badger hair shaving brush was always of great interest; so too was the tasty shaving soap which he licked from the shaving mug. As for the act of shaving, that was a wonderment and he would force his way up close to watch the procedure. There must have been many a soldier who went to the dance with a few shaving nicks thanks to Wojtek's unwanted attentions.

The bear was also fascinated by mirrors. Gone were the days when, as a cub, he had run away, unnerved by the sight of his own reflection. It should never be forgotten that Wojtek didn't know he was a bear; he regarded himself as an equal among equals with his comrades. So it was obvious these night-time revels were just as much about him as anyone else.

Wojtek was not averse to being groomed himself. Anything from a scrubbing brush to a small comb was used to pander to his ego. He considered himself an extremely handsome soldier. He loved to be clean and well groomed, and he was in peak condition when he was living in the camp. His regular forays up trees often left him quite dishevelled but this was quickly put right by his attentive comrades. Wojtek had several batmen working diligently to make him presentable at all times. But being a bear often overtook his 'human' side, and when a muddy puddle looked too inviting to resist he would jump in, undoing all their good work. At this point Peter usually intervened and scolded Wojtek. The bear would stomp off in a huff, but his passion for food and human company always took precedence over hurt pride.

Even in the worst periods of rationing and shortages after the war, there was one commodity the Polish soldiers never went short of – boot polish. Having been in the company of humans for so long and never having shown any interest in boot polish, everyone assumed he would not eat it. And then one day he did. Not only did he smear the contents all over his face and paws, he also got it inside his mouth. Because he had hidden the tin from sight, no one knew how much polish he had eaten, if it indeed was polish. There were all kinds of dangerous substances lying around, a hangover from the war years. Many of these surplus supplies had been left intact since the nearby airfield had been mothballed. The problem was that without the tin the men had no way of knowing precisely what he had eaten. In the end, Wojtek sheepishly volunteered the large, empty tin of Parade Black polish. Surprisingly, he suffered no after-effects.

These were the lighter moments of camp life. There were less pleasant experiences for Poles in Scotland and that was one of the reasons my grandfather visited Winfield Camp so regularly. Jim had a tremendous respect for the Polish soldiers, especially their bravery, fighting qualities and sheer levels of endurance. When I was small he used to say to me: 'If it wasn't for the Poles, you wouldn't be standing here as you are now, free. You owe them everything. Never you forget that.'

It was a strange thing for him to tell a little girl, and, to be truthful, I did forget until my involvement in this project brought it all back again. By then, of course, I had discovered just how much the United Kingdom owes Poland, and I now understand why my grandfather believed the Polish war effort was instrumental in the defeat of Germany. In the Battle of Britain, when the average survival period of fighter pilots was three weeks, it was Polish pilots who fought side-by-side with the RAF.

But my grandfather's viewpoint was not one universally held by the Scots, or indeed, the United Kingdom. Despite the creation of the Polish Resettlement Corps, rampant xenophobia, shamefully fanned by some MPs and officials in the Home and Foreign Offices, saw the Poles traduced as reactionary Fascists for their hatred of Communism. The Poles' anti-Soviet views were not popular among a public still deeply influenced by UK war propaganda which had been highly supportive of the Russians and silent on their treatment of the Poles.

Indeed, no Polish servicemen were invited by the UK government to take part in the official British Victory Parade in June 1946 – save for a last-minute invitation extended to Polish airmen after complaints by a handful of MPs. The invitation was declined, the airmen – who had fought in the Battle of Britain – preferring to show solidarity with their Polish colleagues so roundly snubbed by the British Establishment.

Then, of course, there was the issue of employment. Although there were huge manpower shortages, particularly for coal miners and agricultural workers, trade unions agitated for – and got – a government regulation which forbade potential employers from taking on Polish workers: 'Foreign labour can only be employed when no British labour is available and willing to do the work.'

In many areas this was interpreted by officialdom as meaning vacancies had to be left open just in case British workers might want the jobs at some time in the future. Jobs remained vacant while Poles were forced to search for work further afield.

Clumsy handling of the situation reached its absolute nadir when the Attlee government was forced, following an ill-tempered debate in Parliament, to introduce special guidelines to stop Polish musicians playing at dances and socials. The regulation stated: 'No Member of Polish Units shall play in uniform in public outside the precincts of his camp, whether for a fee or otherwise.'

That mean-spirited ordinance was most certainly ignored in the Borders. Polish musicians regularly played in schools at Christmas time and at dances they organised at the camp. In fact, the local policeman was in the band! School children loved classroom visits from the camp's musical groups, and would giggle when they sang well-known songs and carols in Polish instead of English. The men would play instruments such as penny whistles made from tins and cannibalised war surplus. These often would be left behind as presents for the schools.

But it was the carefully crafted toys which the children, scrubbed clean and smelling of carbolic soap and camphor, their little faces wide-eyed with anticipation, were waiting for. The men would spend months making dolls, dolls' houses, animals for miniature farms, and many other beautiful toys.

In postwar Scotland, a party with entertainment and presents was a welcome break from a life of relative poverty. Many of the children had lost their fathers and older brothers in the war. Shorn of family support, they were being raised by mothers holding down low-paid jobs. Luxuries were non-existent. So a party with entertainment, parcels and sometimes a bear out in the school playground (Wojtek wasn't allowed in classrooms) was almost too much to take in. Those few moments provided memories to be held for a lifetime. Many of the men, of course, had left behind their own children or young brothers and sisters in Poland. For them it was an opportunity to recapture something of the magic of Christmas, as seen through the eyes of youngsters.

The harshness of reality was never far away. Displaced persons in Scotland had to report every fortnight to the local police station. By the time Wojtek and his companions arrived at Winfield Camp in October 1946, in Scotland there was one Pole to every 141 Scottish nationals; in England and Wales there was one Pole to every 322 English and Welsh nationals. And the strains were showing. Only the year before, 800 Polish soldiers had decided to boycott the Scottish Borders town of Peebles and not fraternise with the local population because the local council had asked the government to send them all back to Poland. In Fife a somewhat illiterate poster campaign was launched:

ATTENTION! ATTENTION!
Your Home and Job demands that you
STOP POLISH INVASION NOW.
STAND EASY and you've 'Had it Chum'

In Edinburgh only three months before 22nd Company arrived at Winfield Camp, there were press reports about embittered Polish soldiers creating a disturbance at a public meeting held under the auspices of the British Council, and chaired by the lord provost. They booed and catcalled the Polish ambassador, who was making the main speech, and they eventually had to be ejected by the police.

Fairly typical of the anti-Polish letters politicians were receiving from the public was the following: '. . . it is time they were back in Poland, great lusty fellows simply idling about with nothing to do (but frat with our girls) while Poland needs them now. I am sure you will regret it if you do not act boldly and sensibly and order them to return, they are all without exception anti-Russian and have no good word for our fine, brave allies.'

It was all a million light years away from Churchill's rhetoric when prime minister. In his pledge to the Poles at the end of the war, he told the House of Commons: 'His Majesty's Government will never forget the debt they owe to the Polish troops who have served them so valiantly and to all those who have fought under our command. I earnestly hope it may be possible to offer them citizenship and freedom of the British Empire, if they so desire . . . But so far as we are concerned we should think it an honour to have such faithful and valiant warriors dwelling among us as if they were men of our own blood.'

That ringing endorsement was largely ignored. The UK civil service, numerous organisations, unions and politicians, local and national, and even the military, were keen to repatriate the Poles as fast as possible. Forced repatriation was used, but the UK authorities also employed more subtle methods, tactics extended to the Borders.

My grandfather told me that when the army's top brass discovered that soldiers from the King's Own Scottish Borderers were regular visitors to Winfield Camp they ordered Scots servicemen to encourage the Poles to opt for early repatriation. The KOSB were well aware of what was happening on the ground in Poland under the harsh new Soviet regime. They knew no man returned without consequences and many went back only to be branded traitors. Their fate was sometimes death or imprisonment. With this in mind, the Scots soldiers defied their orders and told the Poles exactly what they knew, soldier to soldier. Some Poles did not believe it and returned to Poland anyway, homesickness outweighing the rumours and warnings. Whatever happened, there were few letters received back in Berwickshire when the men left for Poland. Severe censorship meant it was many years before any record of what happened to them could be traced. Even then the information was pitifully thin.

The idea that Scots soldiers could be used for political purposes, after all they had been through, seemed to my grandfather a slight on them as well as the Poles. It was very clear to him that the politicians of the day knew precisely what was going on in the Poles' ravaged homeland. But for political expediency, the inconvenient truth about life in postwar Poland was kept strictly under wraps while Stalin, who enjoyed the touchy-feely nickname of 'Uncle Joe' in the West, was promoted as the saviour of the Eastern bloc, not its oppressor. It was because of this my grandfather hated the UK's ex-Communist minister for labour and national service, Ernest Bevin, with a passion. When Jim bought his first television in the early 1960s, he would switch it off any time a Labour politician came on. He never trusted any political party or any member of the trades union again, believing that if they could sell out the Poles, they could sell out the military. Yet he had come from the left.

Meanwhile, against this backdrop, proprieties were to be observed by duplicitous officials. There was a battalion of government officials, military advisers and local dignitaries checking on all aspects of the men's welfare. Even the bear had to be given his own medical MOT. Not unnaturally, among the bureaucrats there was confusion when Wojtek's name appeared on the medical list of the visiting doctor, but he knew exactly who Private Wojtek was and called in his friend the vet to give him an examination. State protocol required all the men be given adequate medical attention since many had received wounds and injuries in their military activities; as a serving private, that courtesy extended to Wojtek, too.

Thus the men of 22nd Company found themselves walking something of a tightrope when it came to gaining acceptance within the community. Their officers were punctilious in ironing out any problems which arose and did all they could to develop and cement good relations with the local movers and shakers. To be fair to the Borders, many people liked and accepted the Poles despite being woefully ignorant of their culture. The Poles, perforce, had to learn about the Scottish way of life irrespective of the language barrier and they quickly made up their minds that most Borderers, if a bit reserved, were friendly folk who responded to their overtures. In this regard Wojtek proved a brilliant ambassador. His presence always broke down barriers.

To help fraternisation most rural areas established branches of the Scottish–Polish Society and Winfield Camp was no exception. They held regular functions, had special speakers brought in to address them and they looked after the men's welfare. At one of their meetings it was decided to make Wojtek, whom the newspapers had dubbed the world's most famous bear, an honorary life member. The motion having been passed, the meeting was adjourned so that a delegation could take him a bottle of beer to celebrate his elevation to the ranks of the good and the great.

True to form, Wojtek provided an unexpected finale to the event. Across the road from the camp – and, strictly speaking, out of bounds – was a pond where he had been playing with a tyre, diving in and out of the water and batting it about. Tiring of the sport, he left the pond and leapt out onto the road, straight into the path of a lorry driving past the camp. Swerving violently to avoid him, the shocked driver went nose-first into the pond. That, however, was the least of his worries. Seeing a large, curious bear approaching him, he jumped out of the cab and ran for dear life. Wojtek loped after him. The terrified man, who turned out to be a German former POW, spotted a tree and began climbing it in the vain hope of escaping the bear's unwanted attentions. Naturally, Wojtek followed. He had never treed a man before and was enjoying this new game.

Man and bear climbed higher and higher, Wojtek snorting with enjoyment. With the sort of comic timing worthy of a Charlie Chaplin movie, the delegation, led by a kilted man holding a bottle of beer, put in an appearance. The group stopped dead in its tracks at the spectacle. By sheer good fortune, Wojtek's guardian Peter happened to be among their number and he immediately ordered Wojtek to come down. With a last lingering look at his new playmate, the bear did as he was told.

Even though the odds of finding employment suitable to

their talents were stacked against them, the Polish servicemen at Winfield Camp were excellent traders and quick to exploit any opportunities that did arise. They bartered for additional foodstuffs and small luxuries like soap, trading cigarettes and vodka, the latter which they made in great secrecy in an illicit still. Even today, more than 60 years on, former camp residents won't admit openly that they had at least one still on the premises. They were surrounded by the natural ingredients they needed: grains such as rye (which is used in traditional Polish vodka), wheat and corn. Other substitutes for the distillation process such as potatoes and potato peelings were also easily available and even molasses (used in some animal feeds) were to be had – all coupled with wonderful, clear Scottish water.

Being a country area, there were many ways to get around the shortages quietly. It wasn't exactly the highly organised black market that existed in urban areas, but if someone bagged a brace of rabbits or netted a good-sized salmon from the river there were opportunities to trade for other com-modities. Even Wojtek was known to capture a very plump Tweed salmon, though he consumed most of it before his return to the men.

The camp cultivated its own vegetable patch, which enabled the soldiers to create Polish dishes, much to their private relief. The Poles had difficulty in coming to terms with Scottish cuisine. With the sea virtually on their doorstep, families had access to a regular supply of white fish. Because of that, fish suppers were part of the area's staple diet. Deep fried fish in batter was something the Poles, used to eating carp, had never encountered before. And, frankly, they found it in-edible. Wojtek assuaged their guilt at wasting food – a 'crime' of the first order – by gobbling up the abandoned fried fish.

Although rationing was still in existence, Berwickshire was

a good place to be food-wise, for man and beast. A plentiful supply of eggs, milk and butter meant a great deal of home baking was possible; the missing ingredient, of course, was sugar, although most homes had a good supply of honey which could be substituted. Sugar rationing continued for some time after the end of the war so sweetened condensed milk was very popular. Soldier and home baker alike luxuriated in its intense sweetness and velvety consistency; it was as pleasing to the eye as to the palate. Once a tin was opened, even the lid was carefully scraped of all residues. So precious was even one tin of sweetened condensed milk that Wojtek always was excluded from the secret moment when it was opened. The men mixed the condensed milk with coffee, a concoction that amazed the locals as tea was the staple brew for the Scots. The Polish mixture was deemed foreign, but more than acceptable, and it administered an almighty, and most welcome, kick. Wojtek, however, never got to experience the delicacy that was sweetened condensed milk – it was too highly prized to be shared with even a popular bear. Besides, he had such a sweet tooth that if he had tasted it there was every possibility that he would have torn the camp apart in search of more.

As the months rolled on, a trickle of letters arrived from home. The much-longed-for mail did not always contain good news and much of it was censored. The destruction of so many towns and cities in Poland during the war meant media communications were still limited and the men relied on family and friends for real news. Many personal and tragic stories unfolded.

When the post came, Wojtek, often aware of any change in his comrades' mood, would sidle up to them and pretend to read the meagre pieces of paper in their hands. Used to constant attention, he would normally expose his more childlike qualities in the form of a tantrum or a sulk if he was ignored. But when the letters arrived his behaviour changed. He would sit close beside the recipient, offering the comfort of his great bulk. The letters often contained stories beyond all endurance. Relatives lost or dead, yet joy at finding that one sister or brother, or aunt who had survived by some miraculous act of fate or by the courageous hand of some unknown stranger.

For those who had no good news, Wojtek was always there. Animals living with humans are able to read the emotional language of our bodies rather than the words we utter. And Wojtek instinctively knew when a man needed the comfort of his presence. He just sat close and kept still.

# 7

## Messing About in the River

The sight would have given any self-respecting water bailiff apoplexy: disporting himself in the River Tweed, one of the world's most famous salmon-fishing rivers, was a large and boisterous bear. Even those with the most rudimentary knowledge of such animals know that, when it comes to salmon, bears are killing machines.

At pre-war tariffs, taking a salmon beat for the season cost a small fortune equal to many an annual salary, and the river was rigorously patrolled to ensure non-permit holders and poachers didn't fish its waters. During the war the issuing of licences for the River Tweed was suspended and people fished freely for prime Scottish salmon to augment their food rations. However, bailiffs and local ghillies really didn't approve of uncontrolled fishing, whether netting or angling, and now that the war was over kept a close eye on fish stock levels. They weren't overly keen on exotic strangers like bears invading their domain, either. But the bear in question was Wojtek and he wasn't interested in catching Scottish salmon (well, that's the story they told the bailiffs), he was indulging himself in his second-greatest passion (after food, of course) – the joys of messing about in the river.

The River Tweed was actually only a few yards away from Winfield Camp, across a field, down a narrow road and through a wood to Wojtek's favourite picnic area behind Paxton House. However, with trees reaching right to the river's edge the spot didn't offer the men the room they needed to control Wojtek and his insatiable curiosity. When away from the camp he thought he was back on a march and, although on a chain, he still needed to be kept on open ground.

Getting Wojtek to a suitable bathing spot required transport by lorry along with his swimming apparel and makeshift toys. An outing on the Tweed was not a weekly event for Wojtek but a special treat, so the bear made the most of it, floating on his back, paddling and swimming, and sometimes diving underwater for such lengthy periods that his friends on the river bank thought he'd come to grief. Then up he would pop, to the relief of everyone.

The preferred spot for his river outings was under the Union Bridge, a fairly unknown, but stunningly beautiful bridge so named because it links Scotland with England. Built in 1820, it is the oldest suspension bridge in Britain still in use. It joins Scotland and England from Fishwick to Horncliffe. The river is extremely wide at this point, with low banks that make access easy for bathers. The grounds of nearby Paxton House, dotted with wild flowers, sweep down to the bridge through a canopy of trees, making it a truly idyllic spot even today.

Wojtek quickly got to know the routine for his dip in the Tweed, which involved him being accompanied by a full squad of soldiers. First, an extremely lengthy metal chain was attached to his leg iron. The restraint was heavy, but didn't seem to hamper the enormously strong bear, as he plunged joyously into the water. Although great fun, the outing could be something of a testing occasion for the men as, once in the water, he was always very reluctant to come out. When he was supposed to come back to the river bank the men would haul on the chain to bring him in. Gleefully he would turn it into a tug of war. The bear knew that eventually at least six men would be forced to enter the water and tackle him, mob-handed, to float him back to the bank. Wojtek never really left the water until he was ready. Taking his final 'revenge', he would suddenly sprint from the water when he reached the shallows. Heading straight at the men he would shower them with water, shaking and rolling. The men flew in all directions to escape a heavy soaking. Meanwhile Wojtek would look around with immense satisfaction at the chaos he had caused. If his fun was to be cut short, he reasoned, he would have the last laugh. No matter how often this pantomime was rerun, the proceedings always took the same course – with Wojtek winning paws down.

Wojtek wasn't permitted to go to the River Tweed unaccompanied. It was one of only two places permanently out of bounds to him in his remarkably free existence in the Berwickshire countryside. The other 'no go' area was Win-field airfield.

Situated a mere quarter of a mile from Winfield Camp, Winfield airfield became fully operational in May 1942. The story of its requisition from the farm of the same name by the RAF in March 1941 is worth telling.

While having their lunch one day, Mr and Mrs Fleming looked out of their window to see a conglomeration of military vehicles beside one of their fields and scores of personnel milling around. They were still puzzling over the unusual activity when there was a brisk knock on the door. Standing there was a military official. He took requisi-tion papers out of his briefcase and told the couple: 'You have 24 hours to pack up and leave. Your home and your land are needed by the RAF.' The Fleming family – today safely back in their farmhouse – still have the wartime requisition orders.

During the war years Winfield airfield was in constant use,

day and night, as an RAF training ground. Working in tandem with its larger sister, Charterhall airfield, it was top secret and security-conscious. With chronic shortages of aircraft available to promote the war and defend the UK, its young airmen were required to train as pilots and navigators on obsolete and difficult-to-handle early versions of Blenheims, Beaufighters and Beauforts. Accelerated intensive-training programmes and extremely dangerous night flying meant that the attrition rate was pretty high. Barely a month passed without at least one training fatality. In their first eight months of operations Winfield and Charterhall training aircraft were involved in a total of 97 crashes, many of them fatal. Indeed, Charterhall was nicknamed 'Slaughterhall' by airmen.

Air force historian Jack (J.B.) Thompson, in his book *The Charterhall Story*, commented on the lack of dedicated emergency resources for Winfield: 'Help came in many forms. Observer Corps posts plotted crash positions and bren gun carriers and other tracked army vehicles seemed to appear like magic to transport medical staff and rescue crews over difficult terrain. The benefactors were members of the locally based Polish armoured brigade who always seemed to anticipate the need for their services. Often they would stay on to help in the rescue or subsequent recovery of the aircraft. A serving member of the Charterhall medical team still wonders today just how they always came to be waiting for them on the road nearest to the crash.'

The alacrity with which Polish servicemen responded to flying emergencies was due in part to the fact that they knew their countrymen in 303 Squadron were often based at Charterhall with their Mosquito fighter planes.

Following the cessation of hostilities, Winfield airfield was still in regular use before being allocated to the US air force in 1950. Winfield airfield in the mid-1950s reverted to the UK and in later years was used by the Border Reivers Flying Group. It was also used for special one-off exercises by the RAF right up until the 1970s.

In the autumn of 1946, when Wojtek arrived at Winfield Camp, the prospect of young pilots encountering a bear on their air strip was unthinkable, so a strict 'off limits' policy was imposed by Peter. The men understood that if Wojtek strayed into sensitive areas like the airfield there was a real possibility he would be shot.

There is no record of him ever breaching that stricture, nor did he ever stage a solo swimming expedition despite the fact that, with his keen sense of smell, he would have been constantly aware of the River Tweed virtually on his doorstep and the rivers Whiteadder and Blackadder on the other side of the camp less than a mile away.

The ban on Wojtek's unsupervised swimming in the River Tweed arose, in part, because the sea was close enough for the waters to be tidal and subject to strong undertows and currents. While it was unlikely that Wojtek, who was an excellent swimmer, would ever get into difficulties, Peter didn't want him floating down river. He was a bear with a marked sense of curiosity, and the urge to explore new territory would have been irresistible. Thus Wojtek was always on a long chain as he happily floated on his back in the broad expanse of swift-flowing water that marked the boundary between Scotland and England. Wojtek couldn't have cared less about the ban on solo outings. He was in bear heaven.

Only a few yards away from Wojtek's special swimming place is now the Chain Bridge Honey Farm. Had he survived to see it open he would have been beside himself with excitement – honey was one of his favourite treats.

The lush greenery of Berwickshire was a far cry from the

deserts of the Middle East where Wojtek first indulged his passion for water and thorough soakings in the shower cubicles of ablutions huts. But, as ever, his companions put themselves out to ensure he got plenty of swimming. It was as if he was some sort of Svengali who travelled around the world bending his friends' wills to provide him with all the aquatic enjoyment he needed in his life.

The men pandered to Wojtek's enthusiasm for water sports at Winfield Camp too. They made him a crude outdoor swimming pool from a concrete storage tank. The concrete pool had large metal stairs down which he would descend and swim to his heart's content. Unlike most bears, Wojtek didn't just jump in; he would turn around like a human, grip the guardrails and descend backwards into the water, just as most bathers do. His great pleasure showed as he floated and splashed around, flicking cascades of water onto the men. They were not averse to returning the compliment in noisy water fights that all parties greatly enjoyed.

One minor problem was that the makeshift bathing pool was not secure. The tank had high open rails around it which meant that, if the notion took him, Wojtek could easily climb over them and escape from the pool. True to form, Wojtek turned this into a new type of game and, unknown to the authorities, his 'escapes' happened quite a lot. For the bear, it was all part of the fun: the more he created diversions and outwitted his companions, the more attention he got. His mock flights down the field usually ended in a running battle of wits with the men detailed to look after him. They were all extremely fit, and over longer distances could usually outrun him, possibly because the bear let them. When capture seemed imminent, Wojtek would stop and do a swift about-turn. He would head back to the swimming pool and then suddenly stop to shake himself, drenching his pursuers. Then he would clamber up over the railing and dive back in the pool. Once that was accomplished he would grab the floating tyre that he used as an aquatic toy and mock the soldiers by bouncing and bobbing around the edges. It was a glorified game of water 'tig' and he never tired of it.

Swimming was most certainly one of Wojtek's greatest pleasures; the old concrete storage tank and the River Tweed were both superb for a large bear. He liked to include everyone in his frolics and some of these happy times were captured in photographs which show the incredible affection his companions had for him, and he for them.

Once the aquatic gambols were over, Wojtek did everything he could to dry himself quickly. This even included climbing trees to let the breeze ripple through his fur, creating a wind-blown look. He looked a lot smaller when wet, with his fur plastered to his body, but as it dried his coat fluffed up in the sun and wind, transforming him into a huge, fluffy teddy bear.

One question arises: why did Wojtek, when swimming in the Tweed, never indulge in an orgy of salmon hunting as his grizzly cousins undoubtedly would have? Perhaps the answer lies in two directions: one, he had never been taught how to fish; two, his hunting instinct was not as highly developed as it would have been in the wild because food came fairly easily to him. The salmon can count themselves lucky he was more interested in being a soldier than a bear. However, he did find the odd salmon which were probably exhausted from spawning and were dying in shallow waters.

The men also took Wojtek to the shore at Berwick, for romps in the sea. This he loved too because of its unconfined waters. He would dash through the freezing waves and hurl himself with great abandon at the larger ones which swept over his head. Although he was a bear who hated being cold, he seemed impervious to the rigours of sea-bathing which, in Scotland, is not for the faint-hearted at any time of the year.

As well as visiting the beaches of Berwick, Wojtek and his handlers regularly went to the town of Berwick itself. Only six miles from Winfield Camp, for fit young men itching for entertainment Berwick was something of a magnet. Like frontier towns the world over, it was an exciting place. After the war it was still filled with servicemen of all nationalities on the lookout for girls and a good time. There were fist-fights galore and lots of rowdy horseplay. The demon drink had its part to play, of course.

When Wojtek came to party with his friends in Berwick, he always caused a sensation. It should be remembered that this was an era starved of entertainment as we know it today. There was hardly any TV (very few people had the primitive black-and-white sets), no iPods, no Internet, no shopping malls, no indoor sports halls and precious little in the way of organised sport or dances. However, with its abundance of pubs and hotels it is hardly surprising that, with his fondness for alcohol, there were times in Berwick when the bear grossly exceeded his quota of two bottles of beer on any one day.

One night, when the Poles came to town, Wojtek found himself the star of the show as usual. He quickly attracted crowds of well-wishers, quite a few of whom wanted to buy him and his Polish minders a drink. Partying at the now-defunct Berwick Arms Hotel things rapidly got out of hand. The men had congregated outside the hotel entrance with the bear and were engaged in a very rowdy and boisterous social gathering. By this time Wojtek had consumed countless bottles of beer, as had the Poles, and all were drunk. A Polish officer appeared on the scene to find a group of drunken soldiers with an inebriated bear. None of the Poles were worried by Wojtek being the worse for wear, indeed they were claiming the bear had said his first words that evening when he let out an enormous beer burp! Unfortunately, the officer did not share the joke, and the men were immediately ordered back to camp. Wojtek, like his comrades, suffered a gigantic hangover the next day and things were pretty quiet for most of the week at Winfield Camp as Wojtek's companions served their punishment. Although all were confined to camp for some time afterwards, the incident was eventually forgotten and men and bear were permitted to return to both Berwick town and the Berwick Arms.

Wojtek's regular trips to Berwick were to hopelessly confuse matters concerning the town's semi-official emblem, known to locals as the Berwick Bear, a confusion that exists to this day. Anyone visiting the town is confronted by a profusion of images of the Berwick Bear on plaques, public buildings, websites and even on town council stationery. Many people think it is a reference to Wojtek, but it is not. Although the origins of the Berwick Bear are unknown, it certainly predates him by many years.

Puzzlingly, Berwick's town crest, an official heraldic device, features in its background a bear. Again its origin is a mystery. The accepted explanation is that the crest's designers introduced the bear as a sort of visual pun. By combining it with a Wych Elm, also displayed in the crest, people arrive at an approximation of the name of the town, Berwick. This sounds somewhat convoluted considering the full name of the town is Berwick upon Tweed.

One of the most famous pubs in Berwick is The Brown Bear, but it is not known if Wojtek ever visited it. It is a distinct possibility that he did because the Poles and Wojtek frequented any bar or hotel which would serve them. It seems strange that in a town so populated by Wojtek lookalikes he hasn't been commemorated with a plaque. Because of the times, few photographs were taken but the stories remain of his participation in the revelries of the day. Over the decades the emblem and the actual bear have merged into one and legend has replaced fact.

But then Berwick's history has always been pretty confusing. The ancient town of some 11,000 souls is situated on the border between Scotland and England and the town changed hands between the two countries so many times that those drafting a peace accord to end the Crimean War with Russia couldn't keep up. In 1856 Berwick was omitted from the Treaty of Paris, signed by Queen Victoria. Thus, while the world has moved on, Berwick remained technically at war with Russia until recently, though no-one can clarify. It would have been ironic if the Poles from Winfield Camp had found themselves having to defend this little town against an ancient foe. Just for the record, Berwick is in England now, but cunningly still retains a foot in Scotland. Or maybe a bear paw.

# 8

# Wojtek's Passion for Country Dancing

Picture the scene: it is late autumn in 1946 in the county of Berwickshire where hunting, shooting and fishing are a way of life. It is the open season for game hunting. From the landed gentry in the big house to the farm labourer in his cottage, it is an abiding passion in an area rich in wildlife. A battered old military truck grinds its way along narrow country roads and sitting beside the driver in the cabin is a giant bear, peering anxiously out of the side window. He is looking for village halls and whimpers with excitement every time he spots one of the many small community halls dotted across the rural landscape. Wojtek is going to a dance.

For Wojtek, Scottish country dances were pretty much the highlight of the bear's social calendar. Very quickly he came to associate dances with the small but distinctive buildings where they were held. It wasn't just the smell of the grease-paint and the roar of the crowd when he performed his party tricks, show-off that he was, that drew Wojtek to the dances, or the prospect of making new friends, although that was always welcome. The attraction was the country dances' home baking.

Quite simply, he loved home baking. It was right up there with his absolute all-time favourite treat, cinder toffee. These delicious homemade sweets are known in the Borders as puff candy. Added to the toffee mix are vinegar and bicarbonate of soda which, when baked in the oven, react together, frothing up to release millions of little bubbles into the mixture before it sets. The candy then hardens into something that looks a lot like pumice stone, but tastes a great deal better. Cinder toffee was usually made by the mother of one of the Winfield Camp cooks, and the mere scent of it would send Wojtek into paroxysms of delight. With his keen sense of smell, he could detect its presence over long distances.

For the soldiers of 22nd Company, the dances were a way of letting off steam and getting away from Winfield Camp for a few hours. Being fit, personable young men cooped up in the spartan all-male environment of a DP camp pretty much in the middle of nowhere, they were not averse to meeting young women. And Saturday night is Saturday night.

They were always a well-groomed party when they set off for the evening's entertainment. They may not have had much money but they did have style – and access to a professional camp barber who at weekends was a very busy man. Although hairstyles were limited to military cuts, the soldiers liked to be smart. They varied their haircuts, allowing their hair to grow just a little longer than regulation; more than a few shared a pot of Brylcreem, then much in vogue, and were very dapper. While carbolic soap was standard in the camp, the odd bar of perfumed soap was always put aside for Saturday nights.

Despite postwar shortages and rationing, the villages of Gavinton, Foulden, Hutton, Paxton and Greenlaw still managed to provide a lively calendar of social events most weekends which brought men and bear out on the prowl for entertainment. Wojtek also visited Kelso and Duns – the latter being twinned with the town of Zagan in western Poland today. Duns also has its own Polish war memorial.

Most dances held around Berwickshire in the postwar years were in village halls with outside toilets, no bar, and refresh-

ments offered by the local Women's Royal Voluntary Service
(WRVS) or the Scottish Women's Rural Institute (SWRI).
There were gigantic tea urns, fish-paste sandwiches, pies,
home bakery by the yard, and Slipperene, a powder that
was scattered over the halls' wooden floors to smooth the path
of dancers, if not romancers. It might sound tame by today's
standards – no light shows, strobes or dry ice – but those
apparently sedate dances of the postwar years had every
ingredient needed to excite lust, love, romance and even
violence.

There was one other ingredient fuelling that lethal concoction: a smidgeon of alcohol, usually Polish. Irrespective of
their lack of cash, the Border Poles seemed to have an
inexhaustible supply of vodka or Polish spirit, the latter being
a beverage that could strip the enamel off your teeth. It is
doubtful whether either spirit ever troubled the gaze of the
local Customs and Excise officers. Equally, at dances it was felt
unnecessary to involve the fair sex in such male shenanigans.
The young men – Polish or Scottish – would nip outside to
imbibe their drinks, unencumbered by any feminine disap-
proval. In that regard, there were no differences of nationality.

However, it would be less than accurate to say that there
were no tensions between Scots and Poles at these dances. As
a general rule, nobody minded until one of the Polish
company took the fancy of a local girl and a spurned local
swain took exception. There would be a fight and anybody
from the local doctor to the police would intervene to break
up the fray. Inevitably, the two male admirers would be found
to be a little the worse for drink, but swift measures were put
in place to make sure the conflict was ended as quickly as
possible. For the authorities it was important that locals could
feel safe around the Poles. In this regard Wojtek helped in that
he was a distraction from tensions building up between the

two nationalities. On the whole, the dances helped more than they hindered in building relationships between Poles and Scots, but there was nothing could change the strutting, territorial claims of the indigenous youths against the Polish interlopers, save time itself and hopefully the arrival of a more mature outlook.

Into this milieu Wojtek effortlessly inserted himself – usually, it has to be said, in close proximity to the home baking tables. He was quite shameless and given a whiff of encouragement would lie on his back making sheep's eyes at the women in charge of the provender.

A former cook at Winfield Camp, Mrs Denholm, said: 'He loved pies. At the dances he would be on the floor with his minder Peter, who would tell him, "Don't even think about taking one of those pies." Wojtek obeyed him but you could see the effort was killing him. And it would only last as long as Peter was watching. The bear was kept on a short chain for these occasions.'

She added: 'Not all the locals liked Wojtek. They were intimidated by his size. When the Poles turned up with him unannounced some folks would go out of the hall. But most people stayed. At some dances, he would let children clamber all over him and they would ride on his back. It would never be allowed nowadays. However, these were simpler times and there weren't any of today's rules and regulations on public safety. Wherever the bear went, though, Peter was always with him to make sure everything was alright. One word from him and Wojtek obeyed.'

One of Wojtek's greatest loves was music; indeed, at country dances it was almost as big an attraction for him as food, which was saying something. Nowadays he would have been called a groupie. He especially liked violin music. Violins and accordions have always been the musical instruments of choice in the Scottish Borders, and Wojtek enjoyed the toe-tapping reels, jigs and strathspeys that got the dancers up on the floor. When the musicians started to play he used to bob up and down to the basic rhythm, then after a time he sat down to listen; it was a very odd sight, a giant bear sitting upright on his bottom on the dance floor, his legs splayed apart to keep his balance. Usually there were mounds of crumbs in between his legs, the remnants of the many treats he had managed to beg, but his eyes were fixed firmly on the band. He seemed transfixed by the music. That may very well have been a throwback to his early years, when in the wartime camps the men would provide their own musical entertainment to while away their evenings. Being familiar with music from a young age, he must have sensed from the men that this was a pleasant and enjoyable thing. Thus he eagerly placed himself in the dance halls at a spot where he could fully experience the performance, swaying in time to the beat.

Under the violins' influence he became very calm and settled; indeed, on one dance outing he managed a nap half under the hall chairs which were placed against the walls. He was not exactly a quiet sleeper, as his army colleagues would testify. While asleep, his grunts and snorts, with the occasional wind release from either end, made him a less than boon companion.

Outings were not confined to country dances. Wojtek also attended local opera and amateur dramatics performances. He often dozed off there too and his impromptu additions to the performances were a great source of amusement to the locals, especially the children. But it would be safe to say that he was seldom invited back by the organisers of such events. Being upstaged by a farting bear was just too much for any performer, professional or amateur, to tolerate.

However, Wojtek was not to be denied his entertainment.

The Polish soldiers very quickly realised that Wojtek was a 'babe magnet' and took him everywhere they could. Within minutes of him arriving in a hall, there would be a crowd of young women surrounding the bear, trying to pluck up the courage to stroke his soft fur and being urged on by the Polish soldiers, who would take the arms of the prettiest girls and bring them forward to meet Wojtek close up. Other soldiers would show their 'bravery' by going up to him and giving him a kiss. A former camp member, with a twinkle in his eye that belied his 82 years, recalled: 'Whenever Wojtek was in the hall I always made sure I was standing right beside him. That way I was sure to meet all the girls.'

As a safety precaution, Wojtek wore a light chain when attending civilian functions. At first a neck restraint had been employed, but after gorging himself on fruits and vegetables one particularly fine summer he became too fat for it. His mentor Peter then introduced a leather-lined steel hoop which was fastened to his left hind leg to keep him in check on public outings. When it was first used Wojtek grumbled about the restraint and threw an almighty sulk but eventually came to terms with it. At Winfield Camp it was only used when he bunked down overnight in his quarters and occasionally during the day when Peter was off on military duties. For the most part, as long as someone was supervising, Wojtek was allowed to wander freely around the camp.

Living on a farm, Wojtek was surrounded by livestock in the nearby fields, prime targets for a wild bear, but there is no recorded case of Wojtek succumbing to the lure of the chase at Winfield Camp. He did, however, like to stalk sheep. Creeping along the hedgerows of a field where they were, when he was close enough, he thought it a great joke to leap out and watch them scatter in all directions. But he never pursued them further. Peter would scold him vigorously and

Wojtek would take his telling off like . . . well, a bear, covering his face in mock submission with his paws before risking a peep up at Peter to see if his mentor's simulated anger had subsided. It was very much a case of who was kidding who. But the incidents could have been more serious if they had happened in lambing season when sheep upset by his antics might have aborted in fright. In the lambing season – indeed, most of the year – farmers had carte blanche to shoot any strange dog they saw in the field with their flocks, no questions asked. Sheep worrying is regarded very seriously indeed by farmers and at the sight of an unfamiliar animal in close proximity to their sheep, out would come the shotguns. Would they have shot Wojtek? Perhaps not, but any restraint would not have been for any sentimental reasons. It would simply have been because they didn't have farm weapons of a heavy enough calibre.

At Winfield Camp Wojtek's very presence, as he ambled around, a free spirit, lifted the hearts of many men. In those early months, morale was still high and the Poles weren't above roping Wojtek into a joke that they played on their hosts. It was a hoax which quickly passed into camp legend.

As part of the Polish resettlement training programme, a three-man army assessment team had been seconded to Winfield Camp. Their job was to establish precisely what skills, linguistic or otherwise, the Poles had and to establish training sessions for them. Alongside a sergeant and a lieutenant was a man called Archie Brown.

Archie Brown, who recently died in his nineties, hailed from Boroughmuir, Edinburgh. At the age of 22 he volunteered for service with the Royal Artillery before transferring to the Royal Signals. Like the Poles at Winfield Camp, Archie had seen action at Monte Cassino as well as the war's other military hot spots – El Alamein and Malta. Because of their shared experience of Monte Cassino he had a lot of respect for the Polish troops. They in turn liked him.

One by one the camp's soldiers were ushered in to the team's office for their interviews to establish how well they spoke English and to be quizzed about their family circumstances and any skills they had which would aid them in applying for civilian jobs. The sergeant and lieutenant steadily ploughed through the list. As the last soldier departed, Archie came in and informed his superiors that the Poles had told him there was one more serviceman left to see and that, if the interview panel waited for a minute or two, they would bring him along – a Corporal Wojtek.

'Apparently, he only speaks Polish and Persian,' said Archie, who thought the whole matter rather odd.

'Better wheel him in then,' said the lieutenant, before suddenly breaking off mid-sentence. His jaw dropped, and beside him his sergeant's face turned white. Archie, who was standing with his back to the door, whirled round to see what they were staring at – and was confronted by a giant bear. Corporal Wojtek had arrived. The shaken trio were reassured by the laughing Poles that Wojtek was harmless and a seasoned army campaigner in his own right.

It is rather doubtful whether the bear was officially promoted from private to corporal, although Archie has always insisted that the men called him that when they staged their prank. He said the bear was recorded as a corporal in the NAAFI (Navy, Army and Air Force Institutes) records to ensure he received official rations. Whether the Poles simply elevated Wojtek's rank to give their jape additional credibility, or whether he was indeed in the NAAFI records as a corporal simply isn't known. Whatever the truth of the matter, we may be sure the bear enjoyed his notoriety.

Despite their hatred of the Russians, initially the men in

Winfield Camp clung to the belief that their homeland would regain its freedom and that they would be able to return. The Poles had a touching faith in the integrity of Britain in upholding their rights. However, the truth was otherwise: the political battle for Poland's future had already been lost. Many months before the great powers sat down at the negotiating table at Potsdam, Stalin already controlled Poland through force majeure and he was not about to give it up. Poland had vanished behind the Iron Curtain.

Many Poles at Winfield Camp refused to accept that. They clung tenaciously to the belief that this was only a temporary arrangement and that, when things settled down in the maelstrom that was postwar Europe, Poland would somehow re-emerge as an independent nation.

The authorities in Britain were keen to accept − at least publicly − Stalin's assurances that for the Poles democratic, free elections were on the way. The young soldiers of Winfield Camp were among those encouraged to return to Poland. In the transit camp that Winfield was becoming, some of those who could find their families took the gamble and returned. But the homecoming for many ended in heartache and despair. Some returned to the 'new' Poland only to be shot or disappeared as traitors. Scanty details of these new purges eventually percolated back to the UK usually through news reports from the BBC. Other information filtered back from organisations overseeing the return of troops; they too hinted at many atrocities. Stateless and abandoned as a nation, the remaining Poles fought a political battle behind the scenes to be allowed to remain in the UK.

While that battle was in progress many of the men took the opportunity to visit other parts of the country, prospecting for jobs and a new future. Because of the large number of camps where they could stay, it was easy − and inexpensive − to travel around. Quite often the men would be given official leave to go and visit fellow Poles in other towns or simply to use the time to explore life in Scotland. It was a way of preparing them for civilian life in the Scottish community. Like many before him, Peter decided to explore his options and visit friends. He left Winfield Camp on a two-week furlough. It was the first time Peter had ever left his charge for more than a couple of days, but he didn't expect any trouble.

Leaving Wojtek at the camp was a fairly simple operation. Everyone knew the drill and as the bear knew and was friendly with many of the men there was no great disruption to his daily routine. Even so, Wojtek regarded Peter as his mother and the bear was uneasy when he left. Even though Wojtek would obey and play with the other soldiers, during the brief periods he and Peter were apart Wojtek would mourn his absence either by throwing the occasional tantrum or descending into unusual quietness. This usually passed as other distractions appeared, and the men would cajole him with food or toys such as lorry tyres or footballs to raise his spirits.

The two weeks passed moderately well; there were no real incidents apart from the odd tantrum before bedtime and occasions when he would go walkabout on a hunt for his missing parent. The day Peter appeared back on camp their reunion proved a lot more exciting – and dangerous – than he had bargained for.

At the sight of his mentor, a joyous Wojtek came lumbering towards him and embraced him in a massive bear hug. Unfortunately, Wojtek was so overjoyed by Peter's return that it was a real bear hug, one that came close to crushing the life out of him. The bear had completely forgotten how powerful he was. Poor Peter was close to suffocation: his face began to turn purple and he could feel his ribs start to give under the pressure of Wojtek's embrace. Realising Wojtek was crushing him to death, the men panicked for a second, not knowing how to get the bear to release him. Luckily Peter knew. The only way to stun an unsuspecting bear out of its actions was to hit it square on the nose – its most sensitive part.

Although close to passing out, Peter managed to land a heavy blow straight on Wojtek's long black snout. It was a punch that hurt him as much to deliver as it did Wojtek to receive it but it jolted the overexcited bear into releasing him. In a split second, the joy of their reunion turned to sorrow. Wojtek, eyes watering from the pain and the shock of his master striking him, sat down on the rough dirt track and sobbed inconsolably. He melted into absolute despair; the pain and rejection were too much for him. He was completely unaware he had come close to killing the person he most loved in the world.

Needless to say, Peter, too, was overcome with regret but he'd had no choice in the matter. The bear would have killed him with love. Throughout Wojtek's life there had been very few incidents involving the bear which could have been construed as dangerous. His most redeeming qualities were his mild manners and docile nature.

Peter consoled the broken-hearted beast with comforting words and soothing strokes across his back. Although still shocked, Wojtek recovered from his humiliation, accepting a tasty snack Peter had brought in his pocket for the bear on his return. The relationship restored, life drifted back to normal, but it was Wojtek's last bear hug.

Meanwhile, as weeks stretched into months, the men at camp found themselves trying to survive the boredom of camp life while coping with the growing disillusionment of being left without a homeland and without a future. As 1946 wore on well into 1947, there seemed to be no resolution in sight. Looking back at those days of uncertainty and confusion, Augustyn Karolewski (Kay) said: 'If you had told me 60 years ago I would still be living in Scotland now I would have thought you were mad. I would never have believed you. In my wildest dreams it never crossed my mind.'

Undoubtedly the meeting of the girl who was to become his wife heavily influenced his decision to settle in Scotland. But perhaps so too did the words of his future father-in-law. When Kay went to see him about walking out with his daughter, he was asked, not unnaturally, about his prospects and his ability to support a wife and family. 'Well,' said Kay cautiously, 'I don't really know. I haven't got a job, I've no money, I haven't got a home and I haven't got a country . . .'

'I'm nae interested in your past; that's behind you,' was the blunt response. 'I'm interested in what's in front of you.'

Kay, widely known as a prodigious worker on the farms nearby, quickly took the point. It seems almost superfluous to add that in 1948 he married the girl of his dreams with the full-hearted approval of his father-in-law, and the couple went on to have a family of four.

For Kay, there was to be a happy and successful life in Scotland. For Wojtek the future was much more problematic. He had lived all his life pretty much like a human being. Because of it, he confounded animal experts with his behaviour. My grandfather and other witnesses said you could walk up to Wojtek and look him straight in the eye – which in the ursine world would be interpreted as an aggressive challenge, eliciting a belligerent response. That simply didn't happen with Wojtek. He was very comfortable making eye-to-eye contact and considered it non-threatening.

Equally, his famed dexterity puzzled animal behaviourists. According to his companions, Wojtek could pick up a matchstick from the palms of their hands as swiftly as any human being. Experts say this is impossible – bears aren't physically equipped with that deftness. The fact is, he did these 'impossible' things, and there is no real explanation for them, except from Kay: 'The men had nothing, no possessions, he was all they had. They put everything they had into him and he gave everything back that they needed. He wasn't exploited or forced to do the things he did, he did them because he wanted to do them.'

That statement is indubitably true. But as time wore on things were changing. A new era had arrived and storm clouds were gathering to imperil Wojtek's happy existence. Throughout 1947 the men from Winfield Camp were steadily being demobbed, some to reunite with their families, others to emigrate to Europe, the USA, Canada and Australia, and still more to England, where jobs were more plentiful. With every month that passed the question became more clamorous: what was to be the fate of Wojtek? He was going to be demobbed, too.

After months of vacillation about what to do with Wojtek, a decision about his future had to be made. There was a certain inevitability to it. After years of being treated like one of their own, Wojtek was to revert to being treated like an animal. He was to go to a zoo.

# 9

# The Saddest Day

How do you describe the end of the world? For Wojtek it was a crisp Saturday morning in November 1947. Hoar-frost covered the fields and hedgerows and the frost-rimed corrugated roofs of Winfield Camp's Nissen huts glinted in the weak winter sunshine. It was the sort of morning the bear loved. To the onlookers, his former comrades-in-arms who stopped by his hut to pet him and talk to him, never had Wojtek's thick fur seemed more lustrous and clean-scented. Never had he appeared so content, and so oblivious to the knowledge that this was the day he was to be transferred to Edinburgh Zoo.

At his hut, as usual, Wojtek waited for Peter Prendys to free him from his tether. And as usual, he licked Peter's face, his normal morning greeting to him, while the serviceman undid his overnight restraint for the last time.

In camp the mood was grim. As they watched him amble round to the cookhouse to cadge more breakfast, many of the Polish soldiers were openly crying. The bear had been their companion through years of battle campaigns; he was one of their own. They had faced danger together; they had played with him, wrestled with him, covered up his escapades from the officers and helped scrounge food for him when rations were scarce. From cub to fully grown bear, Wojtek had laid claim upon their affections far more deeply than they had ever realised. Small wonder there were tears. But Wojtek – intent on being fed – for once didn't pick up on the atmosphere. Perhaps that was a small mercy.

For months arguments had raged in the camp about what to do with Wojtek. At times the debates became so heated that the Poles almost came to blows. One faction was holding out for his return to Warsaw Zoo, arguing that Poland would escape the iron grip of the Soviets and eventually life there would return to normal. That viewpoint had considerable currency in the camp although it flew in the face of several harsh realities.

Any hope of 'free' elections had already vanished. More than a few of the Polish DPs at Winfield Camp, anxious to be reunited with their families, had taken the risk of being repatriated to East Poland, only to end up being executed for trumped-up crimes against the State. Others simply disappeared into the Soviet gulag system, or the gold mines of Kolyma in the Arctic Circle, never to be seen again. The privations of Kolyma were so great that to be sent there was considered an automatic death sentence. Nearly all of the Poles at Winfield Camp came from East Poland and had already come to the painful realisation that it was simply too dangerous to go home.

Warsaw Zoo wasn't a realistic option for Wojtek. When Germany invaded Poland, Stuka bombers had devastated Warsaw – and along with it the city's zoo. With most of their animals dead or eaten by a starving populace, during the war years zoo director Jan Zabinski and his wife Antonina had smuggled Jewish fugitives from the Warsaw Ghetto into the zoo's empty cages, hiding them from the Nazis. Others were concealed inside the Zabinskis' villa, only to emerge after dark for dinner and, during rare moments of calm, to enjoy entertainments such as piano concerts.

Jan was also active in the Polish underground resistance,

*Above.* The bear cub in Iraq. *The Polish Institute and Sikorski Museum, London*

*Left.* Wojtek learned good manners early. *The Polish Institute and Sikorski Museum, London*

*Right.* Always looking for food. *The Polish Institute and Sikorski Museum, London*

*Below.* Wojtek playing in the Middle East. *The Polish Institute and Sikorski Museum, London*

*Above left.* A childlike pose always worked. *The Polish Institute and Sikorski Museum, London*

*Above right.* Wrestling was his passion. *The Polish Institute and Sikorski Museum, London*

*Left.* He was adept at climbing but destroyed all trees. *The Polish Institute and Sikorski Museum, London*

Taking stock of his next willing victim! *The Polish Institute and Sikorski Museum, London*

Pretend fighting and showing off. *The Polish Institute and Sikorski Museum, London*

Good manners meant good food. *The Polish Institute and Sikorski Museum, London*

Boarding the *MS Batory* in Alexandria, Egypt. *The Polish Institute and Sikorski Museum, London*

*Above left.* Jim Little as postman in Moniaive.

*Above right.* The author's grandfather leading a remembrance parade.

*Left.* Wojtek at Winfield Camp.

*Below.* Wojtek at Edinburgh Zoo.

*Above* Aileen Orr and President Buzek
at the European Parliament, Brussels in
2011.

*Right.* Maquette by Alan Beattie Herriot.

and had kept ammunition buried in the zoo's elephant enclosure. Further explosives were stashed in the animal hospital. Meanwhile, Antonina, using her own cash, kept her unusual household afloat during the German occupation, caring for both its human and surviving animal inhabitants which included otters, a badger, hyena pups and lynxes. In all, by the end of the war, the couple had saved the lives of more than 300 Jews. More than 20 years later Jan was to be honoured by the State of Israel as Righteous Among the Nations. On 30 October 1968, Jan Zabinski, having been taken to Jerusalem and honoured, planted a tree on the Mount of Remembrance. There is no doubt that the Zabinskis would have been perfect 'parents' to Wojtek had he managed to reach Poland, but it was not to be.

However, back in postwar Warsaw, the couple's former activities were viewed less enthusiastically by the Soviets and the big argument among the Border Poles was about Wojtek's safety in that city. Those who were against him going were certain the Russians would simply kill him. They reckoned that, if they had no compunction about shooting returning Poles who had served with the Allies, they would have even less compunction about shooting a returning bear who had served with the Allies.

As more and more demobilised Polish servicemen passed through the camp en route to building new lives for themselves in other nations, Peter, who in every way was the bear's surrogate mother, grew increasingly desperate. Every avenue he tried turned out to be a dead end. Wojtek may have been an honorary life member of the local Scottish–Polish Society but the bitter truth was that he was homeless too, and no one knew what to do with him. There was no way that Peter and the bear were going to be able to stay together long-term.

With a heavy heart, he eventually accepted the deal

brokered by his commanding officer, Major Chelminski, to give Wojtek to Edinburgh Zoo under strict terms and conditions. These were that the bear would have a home for life at the zoo and would never be moved or transferred, save with the express permission of the CO. The zoo readily agreed. Thus it was that on Saturday, 15 November 1947, Wojtek left Winfield Camp for the last time.

Wojtek's mode of transport was an open truck. As a demobbed bear he no longer qualified for military transportation, so the vehicle had been laid on for him by Mrs Dunlop of Mayfield. As a member of the Scottish–Polish Society, she had been instrumental in helping Major Chelminski work out the deal with Edinburgh Zoo.

Wojtek, who always liked going on outings and looked forward to them, docilely climbed aboard the back. Accompanied by Peter and another serviceman, Jan, he stood at the top of the truck, towering over its cabin, with both massive paws resting on its roof. As usual, when he and Peter were standing together, Peter had one hand on Wojtek's back and the huge beast reciprocated, standing so close that his body was touching Peter's legs. The mutual comfort of touch was probably a throwback to the early days of contact between the two, man and cub. Now it was a gesture of unconditional love and affection between the pair.

For those Polish soldiers who could bear to watch, that was the last they saw of Wojtek as the truck was slowly driven out of the camp by Archie Brown. The pall of gloom over the camp was palpable.

Archie had also been involved in negotiations with Edinburgh Zoo and was very much the correct choice to drive the bear to his new home. He knew just how much the bear meant to the men and could also act as their interpreter. Archie's respect for the Poles was very much a family trait. His eldest brother, who served in the RAF, was one of only two Scots ever given the honorary rank of colonel by the Poles as a mark of their appreciation for his services to the Polish military as a liaison officer and interpreter.

The drive to Edinburgh Zoo took more than two hours and through it all Wojtek surveyed the countryside with his usual great interest, taking in all its sights. For his two companions, wrapped up tightly in their heavy greatcoats to ward off the icy wind, and wracked with sadness and guilt, the truck journey must have seemed an endless purgatory.

Uppermost in Peter's mind must have been how Wojtek reacted when they were separated for a mere two weeks – when reunited he'd almost bear-hugged Peter into the hospital. Now Peter and Wojtek were being parted once more, not just for a fortnight but forever. How on earth would the bear cope? Indeed, how would he cope without Wojtek?

For Peter, giving up Wojtek was like abandoning his own child. It could be said this was the second time he had lost his family. At the outbreak of the war, after Stalin's troops invaded East Poland, Peter and his wife and two of their four children had been shipped out to Siberia by the Russians, leaving behind their two eldest boys. Somewhere in that great upheaval Peter and his family were parted. Details are scanty, but according to a Polish contemporary, Peter's wife managed to journey back from Siberia to the Caspian Sea. She and her two children were then held in a refugee camp in the Middle East. One can only guess at the horrors the three endured on that epic journey; when travelling they would have been constantly on the edge of starvation. On the journey one of the children died.

Now Wojtek and his companions were making this miserable journey to Edinburgh. In the Scottish capital, Wojtek was driven along Princes Street, past amazed pedestrians and

motorists. A showbiz trouper to the end, Wojtek enjoyed the
sensation he was causing.

At Edinburgh Zoo the truck was directed to Wojtek's new
home. Despite having been told that the bear was domes-
ticated, awaiting him was a welcoming committee of zoo staff
equipped with all the paraphernalia they kept on hand for
new arrivals – chains, steel goads and special cages to force
reluctant or frightened animals into their compounds. To
Peter and Jan the sight of a group of strangers, no matter how
well-intentioned, armed to the teeth with animal restraints
must have been heartbreaking. But fortunately they weren't
needed. When the truck stopped, Wojtek quietly clambered
off the tailgate, accompanied by Peter who still had him on his
short tether.

He and his mentor calmly walked into the barred enclosure
that was to be Wojtek's home – or more accurately, his prison –
for the next 17 years. Peter untethered Wojtek from his chain.
As he did so, Wojtek – as was his wont – gave the kneeling
soldier a swift lick on the face, a thank-you gesture to say he had
enjoyed the journey and was pleased his restraining chain was
being removed. His bright, intelligent, button eyes alive with
curiosity, Wojtek set about exploring his new surroundings.
He wasn't upset or disturbed in the least. From a kit bag, Peter
brought out some clothing and an old blanket, all of which had
his scent upon them, and laid them on the ground. A few
minutes later, stifling his tears, he quietly removed himself from
the enclosure and shut the gate. He and the bear were now on
different sides of the bars. The deed was done.

It took a huge effort of will on the part of Peter and his
friend Jan to leave Wojtek. Standing on his hind legs, grasping
the bars with his huge forepaws, the bear stared trustingly after
them as they walked away. Wojtek then settled down to await
their return.

The zoo's director Thomas Gillespie, who was on hand to witness Wojtek's arrival, was later to write in his memoirs, *The Story of Edinburgh Zoo*: 'I never felt so sorry to see an animal that had enjoyed so much freedom and fun confined to a cage.'

It was said that for a full month back at Winfield Camp Peter wept every night over the plight of Wojtek. In truth, his sadness lasted a great deal longer. Having endured unimaginable suffering, this final loss almost broke him, mentally and emotionally.

Peter Prendys was a rather shy, self-effacing man who preferred to keep in the background or on the fringes of his more ebullient comrades' activities. He was meticulous in caring for Wojtek and quietly and without fuss carried out any arrangements required to ensure matters ran relatively smoothly for his charge. But there is little doubt that he was scarred mentally, and indeed physically, by the privations he endured while imprisoned in a Soviet gulag. Rake-thin, he never fully regained a normal appetite, a legacy of the starvation rations he had had to exist on in the slave camps and on the long journey to the Middle East where he would be part of General Anders' army.

He had loved and cared for Wojtek as if he had been his own child. His colleagues, in the months that followed Wojtek's removal to the zoo, learned not to talk about the bear in front of him because at the mention of his name Peter would burst into tears.

The Polish troops always believed that, somehow, Edinburgh Zoo was only a temporary solution. Some time later, at a Polish club in Falkirk, Peter was asked for his thoughts on the matter. For once, tears didn't well up as he told his inquirer: 'In Edinburgh Zoo I know he is safe. Now I have to look after me. Then we will see.' While in Scotland, he never gave up hope that one day he and Wojtek would be reunited.

The bear pined, too. He had always been an immensely clean bear, carefully tending to his ablutions. But now his beautiful silken coat, which previously he had groomed meticulously almost every day, became dull and dusty-looking.

Even so, Wojtek continued to indulge his passion for water sports. In his zoo enclosure he had his own private pool. Certainly, it was a much less grand affair than he would have liked, and it was furred with algae, but in the years when he was fit enough to do so, he swam and played in it nearly every day.

As was perhaps inevitable, the Border Poles made numerous trips from the camp to see Wojtek in his new surroundings. They were encouraged to do so by the zoo, who wrote to the camp asking them to come. In the early weeks, that sometimes proved less than a kindness. Hearing familiar Polish being spoken, instead of the keepers' puzzling English, the bear's demeanour would instantly change and he would seek out the source to discover his old companions.

One of the Polish exiles who regularly visited Wojtek in the zoo was Kay. He used to take his children to see the bear. Augustyn said the keeper had a soft spot for the bear and was quite prepared to bend the rules a little to ensure Wojtek got his much-loved forbidden treats: 'If he knew you were Polish the keeper would deliberately look the other way so that you could throw cigarettes and sweeties into the compound.'

As Augustyn had lived with the bear in the camp, he knew what Wojtek wanted to hear: a good conversation in Polish. It may have been a bit one-sided, but the bear loved to hear people speaking the Polish language.

Augustyn said he always felt depressed when he left the zoo: 'Wojtek was a different animal in the zoo. Though I'm sure they looked after him very well, he really looked fantastic when he was in the camp, running around free and eating what we ate. His coat was shining and his eyes were bright. In camp he was either busy looking for food or sleeping, not much in between; Peter kept him in check and he was no bother.'

That said, Augustyn agreed with the painful decision to rehome Wojtek in the zoo: 'It was the only thing they could have done in all reality.'

Actually, it was a pretty good choice. Situated in Corstorphine, Edinburgh Zoo was created by the Royal Zoological Society of Scotland and occupies a site of some 85 acres. The zoo opened its gates to the public in July 1913, and quickly established itself as a leading institution in its field. In Wojtek's day it was very much at the cutting edge of zoological practice. Today it houses some 1,000 animals and is currently embarking on an ambitious development plan which will take approximately 20 years to complete at a projected cost of £85 million.

For Wojtek there were still occasional echoes of his old life. More than a few Polish servicemen, completely ignoring zoo safety regulations and to the horror of the zoo staff, would climb into the enclosure and challenge Wojtek to wrestling matches just as they had done back in the camp. The bear would respond joyously, revelling in the familiar games he used to play with his friends. There would be fun and laughter. But then it would come time for the men to leave. They would go off. Wojtek would try to follow them, only to find the way barred.

Frustrated, upset and baffled at what was happening, he would go into a deep sulk. He was a highly intelligent animal. All of his life he had received mixed messages from his companions: sometimes the soldiers treated him as one of their own, at other times he would be handled like a small child or domestic pet. Through it all, Wojtek had developed his own very distinct and quite complex personality which suited him and pleased his fellow soldiers. His was a strange amalgam of ursine and human behaviour. But there was absolutely no doubt that, prior to being incarcerated in the zoo, he considered himself to be a soldier living and working among equals. Thus every time the compound gate stayed shut when his companions walked off, it was hurtful and depressing. All of his life, Wojtek had received conflicting signals from the men: sometimes they treated him like a comrade and sometimes like an animal. Through it all, he had ploughed his own furrow, clinging tenaciously to the belief that he was exactly like them. Now, once again, humans were mysteriously changing the rules and he was left on his own.

Gradually, however, Wojtek's jovial personality began to reassert itself, and he started bonding with his regular keepers. It took him at least six months to accept that he was no longer free to wander off, pursuing whatever interest took his fancy. Now, when groups of Poles visited him, he no longer pined when they departed. Indeed, his keepers noticed that a visit from them seemed to perk him up for several days. His memories of freedom never disappeared but visits from his Polish friends became enjoyable rather than upsetting. He began to settle for what there was, rather than what he wanted.

Always a sociable bear, he took considerable interest in the people – and animals – passing his enclosure. He was fascinated by the march of the penguins, a daily event where the King Penguins waddle through the zoo. King Penguins have been a feature at the zoo since 1919, when Edinburgh Zoo established the first breeding programme in the world for captive King Penguins. The spectacle of their daily parade always drew large crowds of children, particularly in the holidays, and Wojtek loved to hear their young voices.

Perhaps the sound reminded him of the school visits he had made back in the Borders or the times children rode on his back during the country dances he loved so much.

Wojtek's old skills never deserted him. At the zoo, throughout his life, he remained a world-class expert in persuading the public to throw him little treats – often gobbling them up, wrappings and all.

Towards the end of his life, Wojtek stuck more and more to his den, preferring to remain inside. Old and stiff, he found comfort in heat lamps and his warm bed. As his health began to fail, Wojtek retreated into his own thoughts.

On 15 November 1963, he was humanely dispatched; his body was cremated and news articles were written. Although his fame by then had diminished, the memory of Wojtek survived. There is a story that he has a grave but I suspect it is a hope rather than a fact, making a memorial even more important. He was 22 years of age – pretty much the average life span of his breed, whether in captivity or in the wild. Indeed, many thousands of Poles did not live to see their 22nd birthdays.

Back in the early 1960s Wojtek had a plaque on his enclosure at the zoo recording his history. The nearby Post House Hotel even had a lounge bar honouring Wojtek. Beer mats and place mats carried pictures of him and there was a wooden statue of a bear standing in one of the room's corners. This particular statue is believed to be owned by Barnardo's now, and used to encourage charity donations. At the zoo, the plaque about Wojtek has long since vanished. Although zoo staff know of the bear's history, visitors search in vain for a public notice indicating his last home. That should be re-medied.

As for Peter, who was 50 years of age when the war ended, there was nothing now to hold him in Scotland. He moved to

London, where he found work as a builder's labourer. There is no record of him ever returning to Edinburgh to see his beloved Wojtek after that. It is very unlikely that he did so; it would have been much too painful for them both.

However, there was to be a happy development for the serviceman. Peter was reunited with his family. He was joined in London by his wife, who was given permission to leave her camp in the Middle East along with her child. It is not known among the Polish diaspora what happened to Peter's two eldest sons who had been left behind in Poland at the start of the war but it is possible that one or both emigrated to Australia, because his grandsons live there.

Peter died in London in 1968. One of his friends told me: 'I believe Peter and the other soldiers who had been close to Wojtek were broken-hearted at leaving him in the zoo. They faced a very brutal choice – the zoo or a bullet. At the zoo gradually Wojtek became withdrawn. Two bears were added to his cage to try and give him company. However, it was human contact that he yearned for.'

That last sentence is a sad, but accurate, epitaph for the Happy Warrior.

# 10

# Bears Galore Send a Message of Hope

And that should have been the end of the story. Time passed, and I feared that even Wojtek would be forgotten. Today most of his army contemporaries are a dwindling band of former servicemen in their 80s and 90s. Even the official custodians of Poland's history can be forgetful. One of the earliest statues ever made of Wojtek, today housed in the Polish Institute and Sikorski Museum, London, is used as a doorstop. It is to be found propping open the door of a small, rather stuffy private reading room used by visiting researchers – a salutary reminder of the fleeting nature of fame.

Yet the legend of Wojtek continues to reach down through Poland's generations. On the afternoon of Remembrance Sunday in November 2008, a memorial service for Polish servicemen who had fought with the Allies in World War II took place in a new garden of remembrance created for the Polish residents living in Redbraes by PC Simon Daley and officers of Leith Police, near Leith Walk, Edinburgh. With the Polish flag fluttering in a brisk November breeze, and watched by a substantial crowd, it was a moving ceremony, some of it conducted in Polish. At its conclusion, completely unexpectedly, children, some with their mothers and fathers, came forward to lay tiny teddy bears around a small model of Wojtek, a maquette created by Scottish sculptor Alan Beattie Herriot. Some of the teddies had tiny red-and-white armbands, Poland's national colours, others carried miniature Polish flags. Watching the children lay their gifts beside the bear was a beautiful moment, a gesture of great simplicity and purity that completely overwhelmed me. I was not alone; there were tears in the eyes of all who witnessed it. I knew then with certainty that Wojtek was destined to be remembered and would continue to enrich peoples' lives.

Long after they were parted, Wojtek offered his old comrades emotional release; the Polish veterans often found it well nigh impossible to talk to their own kin about the privations they had endured during the war years, yet in relating stories about Wojtek they took the first steps towards unburdening themselves of their experiences. At that ceremony I recalled the letters I was receiving from complete strangers who felt compelled to write. One was from a Polish woman living in London, who said: 'I am writing to you because I read about your campaign to create a memorial for Wojtek . . . As a child the only war stories my grandfather told me were about Wojtek the bear. I think that Wojtek really helped to keep him sane during one of the most difficult periods of his life and he had a great deal of affection and love for him. If I can help your campaign in any way, despite being based in London, I would be very happy to do so as I feel that a memorial to Wojtek would also be a memorial to those who loved him and the troops who served with him, including my late grandfather.'

It was one of many letters of support for my quest to raise a statue in Scotland to his memory and to the Polish servicemen with whom he served. The sight of the children placing their little teddy bears (later to be donated to Edinburgh Sick Children's Hospital) by the maquette of Wojtek brought home to me the true significance of my project. Watching them, I knew that Wojtek would continue to be a power for good, improving many lives, spiritually and emotionally.

There is always something deeply moving about Remembrance Sunday. Whether the event takes place amid the panoply of a state occasion or at one of the small cenotaphs dotted around the towns and villages of Scotland, it is a time to honour those who have gone before us, protecting our freedoms and liberties. It is also a time to reflect on the folly, waste and enormous cruelties of war. Many of us come away from such events with a renewed resolve to promote, in some small fashion, greater harmony with other nations. It is as if the slate has been wiped clean and we are being given another chance to leave the world a little better than we found it.

Wojtek, that artful Happy Warrior, had always had a way of eliciting an enormous amount of goodwill and help, often from most unexpected quarters. There was something about the bear which made people open their hearts to him.

In that spirit, I felt certain the Wojtek Memorial Trust would be successful in its aim to raise funds for a memorial statue for the great bear, despite the fact that establishing the Trust required surmounting more than a few hurdles. I have no doubt that there are many more challenges to face.

From the very outset I didn't want Wojtek's memorial statue to be a stiff military figure, nor did I want a cute and cuddly image of what was a very serious attempt to capture a special moment in time. What was more, it had to engage the feelings of both the Poles and the Scots. For many months I had an image in my head of the statue which could do this, but it was extremely hard to define in words. I had been approached by a number of artists and sculptors who wanted the commission, but none, in my view, had really hit the mark. Although they were passionate about the project, I didn't feel that any of those who had approached me truly understood Wojtek's story.

But that was to change. One night, as I sat in my office in

Sunwick Farm after dinner, still wrestling with the images in my head, the telephone rang. It was Alan Beattie Herriot, a sculptor I had heard of, but had never met. He introduced himself and then said: 'This story has been going around in my head since I heard about it. I must do this.'

I don't know where Alan had heard about Wojtek – in all probability his information had come from the flurry of media publicity about Wojtek's life earlier in the year when it was announced I wanted to have a statue created to the bear – but within minutes of talking to Alan, I felt I had found someone who really understood what I was trying to portray. He was on my wavelength. His artistic vision reflected the reality I was trying to capture.

I found myself, in that first phone call, telling Alan about former camp inmate Augustyn Karolewski and the impression he had created in my mind as he talked of the men walking down the road with Wojtek in front of our farmhouse. When they stopped, Wojtek stood and waited too. All Peter Prendys, or any of the men who handled him, had to do was to place a hand on Wojtek's shoulders and he would stop and stand there. If there was a conversation taking place, the bear would remain on his hind legs, waiting for it to finish. While keeping a weather eye out for any possible food opportunities, or possibly an adventure, he was simply another soldier waiting for his companions. But in the main he would stand like a dog waiting patiently for the command to walk on.

I explained to Alan that the whole legend of the bear was based around his composure and his almost human under-standing of situations. Gossip being exchanged by his mentors may have meant nothing to the bear, but his patience and good manners meant he was given a great deal of freedom whilst staying on the camp. Sunwick farmhouse was always within sight, so the men from the farm were no strangers to

Wojtek. Equally familiar from the other side of the camp were the Fleming family from Winfield Farm. They had been uprooted when the RAF commandeered their farmhouse and grounds for the new Winfield airfield at the beginning of the war, but after its conclusion they had returned to start farming again. Though they didn't anticipate having a bear around their livestock, like everyone else locally, they knew and understood what this bear meant to the men of Winfield Camp.

When I came off the phone, I researched Alan's career on the internet and was mightily impressed by what the art world had to say about him. Alan is regarded as one of Britain's best and most successful public sculptors. His distinctive works in bronze have won him acclaim across the United Kingdom, France and Holland. Working from his studio at Howgate, near Penicuik in Midlothian, Alan is an artistic all-rounder – as well as being a first-class sculptor he is also a highly talented painter and has a strong interest in the portrayal of Scottish history. Wojtek is part of that history.

There are several important Alan Herriot public sculptures in Scotland, including one of another animal who served with the military: Bamse, the St Bernard mascot of Norway's World War II resistance forces in Scotland, who were based in the east coast town of Montrose.

In that first conversation we had talked about Alan's statue of Bamse. I was familiar with the story, having read the book about him. Before his death in Montrose, Bamse had lifted the morale of the ship's crew, and had become a kenspeckle figure to the local civilian population. When standing to battle quarters, he would take his place on the front gun tower of the Norwegians' ship, kitted out in a metal helmet the crew had specially made for him.

There were some striking parallels in Wojtek and Bamse's

'human' behaviour. Like the bear, Bamse was capable of acting without supervision and didn't need to be ordered around. His was a peace-making and morale-boosting presence. Once he saved the life of a young Norwegian officer who was under attack from a man wielding a knife. Bamse pushed the officer's assailant into the sea. On another occasion the dog rescued a sailor who had fallen overboard by leaping into the water and dragging him ashore.

He was legendary for doing his rounds of the town and gathering up his Norwegian companions to take them back to their ship when they were the worse for drink; similarly, he was well known for breaking up quarrels among his shipmates. Witnesses said he would rear up on two legs and put two massive paws on their shoulders to calm them down. He was quite well travelled, too. He hopped on local buses unaccompanied, and would regularly make journeys to Dundee where he would get off at the bus stop nearest to his crew's favourite public house, the Bodega Bar, and go in to fetch them back before curfew. His shipmates even bought him a bus pass, which they attached to his collar, to allow him to carry out his patrols. If Bamse couldn't find his shipmates he would simply take the bus back to base.

At the end of our conversation I put down the phone feeling elated and excited; an artist who already had experience of capturing the essence of a well-loved animal in the military for a public statue was likely to produce something of great artistic merit. And so it transpired.

Within an hour of our telephone conversation, Alan had faxed over an image he felt summed up everything I had told him. I was delighted with the sketch; in a matter of minutes he had achieved what I had been wrestling with for months. Many locals remember well the sight of a soldier and a bear walking down the long straight road to Sunwick – a stretch which was used by the late Formula One racing hero Jim Clark, a local farmer and another local legend. Alan depicted the two as wandering figures, the soldier with his hand on the bear's back, casual, peaceful but not at the end of their journey. The memorial will be their journey's end, a new gathering place for all Poles in Scotland, a place to think and wonder.

A few weeks later I visited Alan at his studio to see a plasticine model which he called a starting point. It was stunning. Alan's studio is lit on three sides, but that day when I walked in, a beam of light streamed down on the maquette, illuminating it alone among all the other works of art. I could see instantly the model worked on a level far beyond my expectations. The power and grace of the relationship between man and bear were magnificent. There were a few minor modifications required, mostly at Alan's insistence. The greatest change was his decision to remove the soldier's helmet and have him carry it, which is what the men would have done in real life. The effect of that modification alone was dramatic; it somehow made the whole scene more compassionate.

The next time I saw the maquette it looked like a bronze cast. But when Alan handed it to me, it was as light as a feather. This was to be my sales aid in raising the funds to cover the cost of the final work. Back home my husband, Andrew, who has an eye for good artwork, was equally impressed. His approval was important to me because I had never discussed with him the representation I had had in my mind's eye. He was seeing the maquette for the first time and if it worked for him then I knew we were on the right track.

But there was one other person whose endorsement was absolutely vital – Augustyn Karolewski, the Pole who had

recounted to me so many Wojtek anecdotes. He had been at
Winfield Camp and had lived the story; Kay, as he is known
to us in the village, had to like it or it would all have been for
nothing, or, at the very least, it would be back to the drawing
board for Alan and myself.

Kay, for an unconscionably long time, observed the figures
of man and bear. Humming softly to himself, turning the
model this way and that in his large, work-calloused hands, he
carefully scrutinised every detail. Perched on the sofa, I tried
to read his face as he pondered over the maquette. The wait
was excruciating, even though I sensed Kay, mischievous man
that he is, was deliberately prolonging the moment. Eventually, after what seemed like hours, he gave his honest
approval and expressed his liking for the whole thing. His
only criticism was that the word 'Poland' had to be included
on the soldier's lapel badge, a detail which Alan was delighted
to accommodate.

With the maquette to everyone's satisfaction, it was now
time for me and my supporters to turn our attentions to the
not insignificant matter of formally setting up a charity,
finding trustees and finding funding. However, other events
interposed themselves.

The maquette's first public outing was to Biggar Museum
in South Lanarkshire, in September 2008, to launch the
Wojtek Memorial Trust. The museum had mounted a
first-rate exhibition about the life and times of Wojtek,
including rare black-and-white pictures of the bear interacting
with his soldier companions. For that display we had to thank
the energy and drive of Biggar Museum's young and enthusiastic museum supervisor Suzanne Rigg. Her research had
unearthed a great deal of interesting material that, coupled
with Suzanne's sunny nature, predicted the exhibition launch
was going to be an enjoyable experience. As guests of

Suzanne, her mum, co-worker Janella Glover, and museum chairman James Dawnay, Alan and I went along to the opening and the night proved a great success.

This was the first time either of us had made official speeches about the project, and we both found the experience surprisingly emotional. I suppose it was because we realised how closely people identified with what we had done. We were also slightly unnerved by the reaction of the very first member of the public to view the maquette: on seeing it, the woman burst into tears. The beauty of what Alan had captured evoked an immense depth of feeling among Poles which never ceases to amaze me. First there is a sense of shock on their faces at the sight of the two figures together and then their features soften as memories flood in. Almost timidly, their hands reach out to touch Wojtek. Even in model form, the bear weaves a potent spell; people cannot stop themselves from stroking his head and ears. Both Alan and I still get huge satisfaction out of watching people's reactions to the model.

Biggar Museum was an important, and appropriate, starting place for the launch of the Wojtek Memorial Trust. Camps in nearby Symington and Douglas hosted a large contingent of Polish soldiers during the war years.

After the launch, time seemed to flash by without much being accomplished. I thought things were going quite well but I was deluding myself. It wasn't until I sat down and took stock that I realised how much there was to do. Television, press and radio interviews concerning the bear were all very well, but fully establishing the Trust and appointing suitable trustees seemed as distant as ever. Having allowed myself an official panic, I pulled myself together and did what I am trained to do (among other things, I'm a qualified accountant): I wrote a professional business plan for the Trust. My first task was to find trustees who understood the story of

Wojtek in the same way that Alan had. He, of course, had already been co-opted to the cause. My husband Andrew assured me that trustees would turn up when I least expected it, and so they did.

The first was Krystyna Szumelukowa, a board member of Edinburgh World Heritage and an international elections observer for the United Nations. She was someone I knew by name, but had never met. Government minister and MSP Mike Russell, to whom I was then political advisor, was giving a speech to mark the start of the annual Polish Cultural Festival in Edinburgh, and I also attended. The event was crowded, colourful, lively and noisy. Large numbers of exuberant Poles and their friends turned up and everyone enjoyed themselves.

As we moved down one side of a stairway in the Queen's Hall in a slow, human wave, Krystyna was being swept upwards along the other side. Mike introduced us almost in passing, saying I was the founder of the Wojtek Memorial Trust. Krystyna looked at me in disbelief, and when I said Wojtek had lived on our farm, she caught my arm with both hands and shouted: 'We've got to meet,' before being swept away in a tide of people. She may not have known it then, but I knew I had my next trustee.

As I was quickly to learn, Krystyna is one of those highly energetic people who have many strings to their bow, as well as a huge array of invaluable international contacts. Born of Polish parents, Krystyna's father was a paratrooper in the 1st Polish Parachute Brigade based in Fife, having made the epic journey from his home in Wołyń via Siberia, Iran, the Middle East and South Africa. Her mother was displaced from her home near Lublin to a farm near Hamburg, from which she was liberated by Scottish soldiers. Krystyna, herself, was born in Germany; the family came over to the UK as part of the Polish resettlement programme.

For more than two decades Krystyna has been developing links between Poland and the UK. She was instrumental in establishing local government and business links between Humberside and Gdansk, Gdynia and Elblag; she helped establish the Edinburgh–Kraków partnership and built charitable links between Marie Curie Cancer Care and the St Lazarus Hospice in Kraków. The Fields of Hope (*Pola Nadziei*) campaign she worked on is now being adopted by 37 hospices throughout Poland. For these and a host of cultural projects, Krystyna was awarded the Polish Silver Cross of Merit in 1999. She currently has business and planning interests in Poland which build on her personal career in town planning and economic development.

Shortly after the festival, Krystyna and her friend Jennifer Robertson came to Sunwick Farm for lunch. Jennifer, a Scot with a lifetime interest in Poland, speaks fluent Polish. As well as living in Poland for several years she has travelled quite extensively in what is now West Ukraine, Peter Prendys' homeland.

Sunwick always looks at its best when bathed in sunshine. The house, itself, is quite distinctive, having been built out of red bricks brought over as ballast in the Dutch ships that plied their trade at the port of Berwick. Indeed, for Poles unfamiliar with the terrain and trying to find their way back to Winfield Camp, the farmhouse was their main landmark. Even if they couldn't always make out directions delivered in a strong Borders accent, when they sighted the red brick house they knew they were close to home.

After a long lunch, talking in the main about the men and Wojtek, we walked down to the camp and to the irrigation pond which had once been Wojtek's swimming pool. Some of the surrounding trees, now mature, still have the scars of Wojtek's razor-sharp claws. Although Wojtek's activities were usually terminal to trees, the odd one has survived. After our tour I asked Krystyna if she would become a trustee, and as usual, Wojtek worked his magic. She accepted and we moved on to find our next victim.

From early in the project, I had regularly sought the advice of family friends, both of whom are Scottish advocates. From them I got an excellent grounding in the legal realities of establishing a Trust: once I had been interrogated as if in a courtroom and had survived a merciless grilling I knew I was going to succeed. Then the more gentle-natured Brian suggested Cardinal Keith O'Brien, archbishop of St Andrews and Edinburgh, would make an excellent trustee. It transpired that Cardinal O'Brien had actually conducted the funeral of General Maczek. He very kindly accepted my invitation. Including Alan Herriot as advisor, that made four of us. But we needed one more for a very solid committee.

The final trustee could be said to have been jointly selected by Krystyna and Wojtek. On one of the many days the maquette accompanied me into the Scottish Parliament, Major General Euan Loudon, chief executive of the Edinburgh Military Tattoo, was standing in the main reception. He approached, asking if this was Wojtek, the famous bear that he had heard about from Krystyna. Once again the bear did his stuff. By the end of our conversation, the Major General had agreed to consider being a trustee. Krystyna followed up on that pledge, and with her on the case, the Major General was co-opted in Wojtek's inner circle. Thus the Wojtek Memorial Trust finally came into being.

From the beginning, I wanted the Trust to be fresh, outward-looking and imbued with a vision of enhancing current relationships between Poland and Scotland through trade, culture and education. There has been no shortage of ideas from the trustees, and as these grow we are now looking at creating memorials in Poland and Monte Cassino as well as Edinburgh. Equally importantly, we hope to dovetail into groups with the same aims as ourselves, and we are finding potential new allies almost daily. It is a very exciting time.

On Wednesday, 25 March 2009, Wojtek was given his own diplomatic reception in the Scottish Parliament, hosted by the presiding officer Alex Fergusson. The presiding officer, himself a farmer, was intrigued by the story and understood immediately its potential impact. The idea for a reception first came from Linda Fabiani MSP, who was then culture minister, and who had a great interest in Monte Cassino, having just been made Cavaliere dell'Ordine della Stella della Solidarietá Italiana (Knight of the Order of the Star of Italian Solidarity) for her work promoting relations between Scotland and Italy. My own boss, Mike Russell MSP, was equally enthusiastic. He thought the relationship between our two countries had long been neglected and he too saw an opportunity to open up historical links. The Wojtek project quietly moved around the Parliament, and I found that people were beginning to approach me on every aspect of Poland and Polish events. Wojtek, it seemed, had taken me in a completely unexpected direction as a fighter for Polish rights. It was new territory but I tried to help where possible.

The decision to hold the reception at the Parliament got some attention from the print press. The story then moved onto TV and became quite a hot topic. Polish journalists were astounded when news reached them that the Scottish Parliament was having a reception for a bear. Wojtek was a legend among Polish families living in the UK but was not widely known in Poland, so many Poles, particularly the younger generations, were hearing Wojtek's story for the first time.

The Polish media coverage brought to the surface new anecdotes about the bear. It also sparked off a number of serious interviews concerning Polish soldiers and their time in Scotland.

Yet more information about Wojtek and the Polish men's experiences in Scotland emerged at the reception. Meeting new people and networking in the crowded Garden Lobby, the main reception area in the Scottish Parliament, I realised that the bear was a superb ambassador, promoting fresh ties between Scotland and Poland. Adding to the mood of the evening, Biggar Museum had brought along their Wojtek exhibition, including a montage of photographs on a video loop – the pictures supplied by Vic Baczor who runs the excellent Wojtek the Bear website. Guests were also shown a display of wartime Polish uniforms, provided by Sean Szmalc and Margot Corson. Many of the old soldiers present enjoyed seeing and touching those uniforms again and they reminisced about its stiff, uncomfortable serge, which they recalled was much heavier when wet, and incredibly hot to wear if they were carrying out any manual work.

In the aftermath of the reception, when the dust had settled, all the thank-you notes had been dispatched, and the phone calls had been made, I found myself reflecting on the journey on which Wojtek had taken me. It was a personal odyssey that started out in childish innocence and a trip to the zoo and culminated in a new way of looking at the world which will forever remain a part of my life. I had not expected that. Very late in my research I realised how lucky I had been to see him in the flesh. He was, and still is, my bear.

I can understand the pain of the men who were forced to leave him in Edinburgh Zoo that fateful day and consign him to a life behind bars. Although it is easy to like the story of Wojtek, his was a journey that contained many, many dark passages. I must confess that as my research progressed and I gained greater insights into Wojtek and his character, I became very proprietorial about the bear; I found it difficult to share him with others and wanted him for myself. However, the simple truth is that the bear wouldn't let me. Gregarious soul that he was, Wojtek loved people and they responded to that.

While I have always been pretty relaxed about the politics of friends whose views diverge from mine, I have never seen a story like that of Wojtek which has inspired so many folk of different political persuasions. And yet, Wojtek may masquerade as a good news story, he may even seem to be a tale offering political opportunity, but those who would use him to their own advantage get short shrift. He keeps me on the straight and narrow.

Through Wojtek, I have been given a radical reawakening to the real-life effects of bad influences of bad government run by bad politicians. Once made, mistakes are very difficult for future governments to rectify. So many people, postwar, were dealt a very cruel hand. That the majority of them have not descended into bitterness, but have had the grace to forgive and build new lives for themselves speaks volumes about their fortitude, resilience, dignity and humanity.

On a purely personal level, Wojtek has done one other thing for which I will always be grateful. In the course of my researches I have met and got to know well many members of the Polish community in Scotland and those communities so ravaged by war through others such as Peter de Vink and Richard Demarco. As their parents and grandparents were cut off from their families during World War II the second and third generations were similarly cut off from their heritage. Through Wojtek, they have been given an opportunity to regain it. My husband Andrew's cousin, Christine Zajack

(Cooper), who had never truly examined her dual heritage, is now doing so because of Wojtek. Her Polish father, Marion, married into my husband's family and sought to assimilate into his new culture as a Scot, which he did very successfully. In the process, he left his Polish past behind him. Christine, who attended the Wojtek reception, found herself discovering a new multiculturalism. An emotional gap that she was hardly aware existed was being filled. Roots are so important; they define our being, whether we like to think so or not. For many, Wojtek has played a part in a healing process.

In ancient cultures in many parts of the world, bears have often been objects of worship. Of these customs, the one that most intrigues me is the celebration conducted by the clans of the Nivkh, a semi-nomadic group living in the trackless wilderness of the Russian taiga. The Nivkh are mainly fishermen, hunters and dog breeders. Bears are considered a sacred earthly manifestation of Nivkh ancestors. Young bears are captured by a Nivkh clan and brought back to the clan's encampments. There the bears are kept in a corral or wooden hut, often for years, tended by the womenfolk. At the time of the bear festival, two clans meet up for a lengthy series of entertainments, culminating in an elaborate religious ceremony in which a bear is dressed in sacred regalia and honoured by being given a last special meal. It is then killed and eaten at a banquet. According to the Nivkh belief system, the bear's spirit then returns happily to the gods of the mountain and rewards the Nivkh with bountiful forests teeming with game. The bear festival is a way of cementing the relationship between two clans already bound by inter-marriage. Wojtek would have liked that, I think, apart from the bit about being eaten. He always enjoyed a good party.

None of us knows where the path of life leads. As we step forward into an unknown, but optimistic, future, I would hazard a guess that Wojtek, in his joyous, mischievous way, has a few surprises in store for the trustees of the Wojtek Memorial Trust. That's as it should be. Any bear who can engender love and respect between fellow human beings is entitled to a little fun along the way, not to mention the occasional cigarette and bottle of beer.

Meanwhile, Wojtek's journey continues, and will do until we find his true home, re-united with his fellow comrades, living in true freedom and enjoying his independence. The Happy Warrior in Bear Heaven.

# 11

# Journey into the Future

There is no doubt that since the Wojtek story became intertwined with my own life, all kinds of coincidences and odd happenings have occurred. In May 2011, I stood in Dumfries as a candidate for the Scottish Parliament. Making my way back to Edinburgh from the constituency in the car on election day, I tucked my candidate's speech for glorious success, or otherwise, inside a copy of my Wojtek book. At that point I still didn't know the outcome. Just as my husband Andrew was driving across the Kingston Bridge in Glasgow, I received a phone call from HQ: all the signs were that I had not made it into Parliament. In the event it transpired that, while putting up my party's vote, I missed my goal by a bear's whisker. Failure is always painful.

As I talked with HQ, my book and the speech fell off my knee and rolled over my feet onto the car mat. The book fell open at the following passage: 'I found myself reflecting on the journey on which Wojtek had taken me. It was a personal odyssey that had started out in childish innocence and a trip to the zoo and culminated in a new way of looking at the world which will forever remain a part of my life. I had not expected that. Very late in my research I realised how lucky I had been to see him in the flesh. He was, and still is, my bear.'

Staring at that passage I had a moment of great clarity: I knew my destiny was staring me in the face, and that any political adventure I embarked upon was destined to be with 'my bear'. Wojtek was always going to be the centre of attention, not my own political ambitions.

It was this realisation that led me onto a new road with Wojtek and the Wojtek project. He had crossed so many frontiers, I felt compelled to do the same, perhaps not geographically, but certainly in piercing the veil of political expediency which had resulted in a total shutdown in communication by so many Poles who had stayed on in this country. Their lives and their pain had not been validated in any way. Initially, I thought the past was too painful, or too distant, for them to reminisce with a total stranger. But digging into the government papers from that time, I unearthed a darker side to the Wojtek story. My research initially raised the fact that the Poles had been excluded from virtually all the postwar celebrations; but much worse was the cosy club which had been formed politically in the UK to expel the Poles from the country, a state of affairs which lasted until Poland's entry into the European Union. The fear of expulsion, I realised, had not just started in the postwar years. Many of the demobbed soldiers lived in terror of 'the knock at the door' for much of their lives. That may seem a lunacy to UK citizens innocent of pogroms and poverty. But after seeing at first-hand expulsions of African and Asian families from Scotland by the UK Border Agency I realised how deeply the Poles must have worried about their future and had little sense of security until they became UK citizens.

For postwar Poles, the road to UK citizenship was always a difficult one; for a long time after the war they were still being pressurised to return home Gradually, the pressure eased, but those who stayed chose, in the main, to live a quiet life as free from controversy as they could. The sadness of this though was the waste of so much talent – surgeons and miners alike took menial work when their skills were so needed, but petty jealousy and prejudice seeping out of the corridors of power, helped ignite a wave of fear which suited so many.

After my research, I now understood why those Poles, living in a free and democratic country, had been so reluctant to speak out. They had never practised the art of free speech, they had self-censored their history, indeed their very existence; their freedom to express themselves as they really were came through Wojtek, a free spirit if ever there was one.

The intention to commemorate Wojtek in the form of a statue depicting him in the company of the Polish soldier has had to weave its way through the protocols determined by the policies and practices of so many institutions and agencies. Finding the right location in the city centre of Edinburgh has seemed at times like a walk through a maze with its many dead ends. Politely I explained that suggestions for the statue to be erected in Edinburgh Zoo was the antithesis of my mission: this was not the freedom that was being sought for Wojtek.

Edinburgh had already adopted, many years previous, a small free spirit called Greyfriars Bobby, who sits on a plinth which raises him to eye-level on the bustling thoroughfare at Greyfriars Kirk. He is usually surrounded by visitors, and well into the night the flash of cameras and mobile phones light up the little dog, who still looks attentive and on duty, waiting for his master. In the case of Greyfriars Bobby, his story is fixed in the mid nineteenth century. He was cared for and fed by the people who lived around Greyfriars and he became a national icon because of his faithfulness to his dead master. Right up until his own death, Bobby had guarded the grave of his owner, John Gray, for some fourteen years, refusing to leave the spot where his master was buried. During Bobby's tenacious daily vigil, local citizens raised many of the same concerns regarding the little dog's fate as were later raised about Wojtek. A case of history repeating itself.

It was argued that Bobby was essentially a stray and should be put down; however, like Wojtek, he had friends in high places, and it was one of these, Sir William Chambers, who paid for the little Skye terrier's dog licence, which allowed him to stay free and alive. On Bobby's death a memorial was erected close to the churchyard gates where he was buried. It was paid for by Baroness Burdett-Coutts, such was her admiration for the dog. Bobby was described by his supporters as the most faithful dog in the world, an irony not lost on us: some 140 years later we are trying to erect a memorial to the most faithful bear in the world within the very same city. Who in all conscience could deny Wojtek his place in the streets of Edinburgh? Like the little dog, he knew freedom in Scotland; he was admired and loved by its citizens as well as the Poles; his life, too, was captured in photographs, and albeit very briefly in war records. Wojtek's journey was that of any soldier heading for battle, and then the long road home. But where was home? Persia, Poland or Scotland? So many places claimed him, yet at the same time he was homeless and stateless. And Edinburgh *was* his home for many years.

The saddest difference between dog and bear is that Wojtek has no grave, as Bobby has. His memory will have to live on in the memorial, and it is there that people will come to lay flowers, as they do for any lost soldier. There is a great deal of love still for the bear from the past, but my real mission is to maintain the story for future generations so that it can be passed on, secure in the knowledge that from the horrors of war true friendships and loyalty can endure. The bond between man and beast can be a force for good, even when arising from the most dire circumstances. Like Greyfriars

Bobby, Wojtek learned to accept the company of humans. When left in the zoo, yes, it must have seemed foreign and lonely at times, but like Bobby, Wojtek had food and company to see him through the coldest and darkest days, even if it was just visitors coming to stare and admire.

There were very few agencies initially who understood the need to remember Wojtek, but when comparing his story with Bobby's, the lightbulb moments occurred. In many ways, Bobby has helped Wojtek through his initial journey for recognition, and the dutiful dog and the loveable bear will always enjoy immortality as their two stories entwine over the years.

Greyfriars Bobby was immortalised in a life-size sculpture created by William Brodie in 1872. I have maintained from the outset that Wojtek has the same appeal. His is a real story of trust and loyalty too. Both animals are undoubtedly part of the story of Scotland, and in indelible fashion, they tell us a great deal about our country in a way that the comings and goings of kings and queens and the good and the great do not. In brief, they fire the imagination.

The summer of 2011 rolled on and I attended book signings, parties and meetings. Wojtek would not rest, nor would he let me sleep in peace either. It was while attending our neighbours' wedding in Kelso, looking over to Springwood Park, Wojtek's first home in Scotland, that I was introduced to Scottish MEP Catherine Stihler. I mentioned I was planning to go over to the European Parliament to talk to Polish members about Wojtek. She was enthralled by the story, and I gave her a copy of the book to read while on holiday. True to form, the artful bear stole her heart and she helped me organise a two-day visit to Brussels.

In early October 2011 I flew over to Brussels to meet President Buzek and attend a large reception in the European

Parliament. At the time, Catherine was heavily pregnant and unable to leave Scotland. I was completely in the hands of her European assistant Pascale Lamb and her Scottish assistant Sonia Campbell, neither of whom I had ever met before, to guide me through the visit. I need not have worried; the diary was full and I had to hit the ground running. To say it was a manic two days is an understatement, and the pair had organised my trip down to the last cup of coffee.

My first visit was with Ian Campbell, Head of Office in the Scottish Government's EU Office. I have always loved the look on officials' faces when confronted by a woman who wants to talk to them about a bear, but Ian was very gracious. Of course, once the story is told, there is complete understanding, and the Wojtek mission is certainly a wonderful opportunity to expand the links between Scotland and Poland. After a very interesting meeting with Ian Campbell, Pascale and Sonia whisked me off to Richard Demarco's 'Scotland in Europe' exhibition. Normally, I run into Richard at art exhibitions in Edinburgh, but as he, too, is interested in the Wojtek story, it seemed appropriate we should meet in Brussels. Richard said: 'You don't have to sell the Wojtek story, Wojtek sells himself,' and he is right. Wojtek is always a current story, fresh and hopeful. Richard gave me a personal preview of the work he was doing and, having such important cultural links with Polish art and theatre, Wojtek fitted in very well.

After dinner I had a quick walk around Brussels before retiring for the night. All too soon it was morning and a hair-raising taxi ride, in rush hour, from my hotel to the parliament ensued. Although prepared, I was unusually nervous. I had met many senior politicians before, heads of state, even royalty, but there seemed to be a feeling of urgency, as if a lot were riding on this meeting. I had no idea if the president had any interest at all in Wojtek, or, indeed, if he knew of the story.

The girls marched me down the long, carpeted corridor to the president's office. He was charming, warm and welcoming. As a Pole, he was fascinated and quite moved by the story. At one point when I was talking about the men, and Wojtek, on the camp, I felt I wanted to cry, which took me by surprise as I am not noted for being a highly emotional type of person. The moment passed, unnoticed by anyone. I noticed that the president had picked up the photograph of Wojtek and was speaking to it, quietly and sombrely, in Polish. So many people listen to Wojtek's story, but when you see a Pole hearing it, it is different; it is deeper, more intense, sometimes overwhelming. It is like flicking a light switch and seeing the bear for the first time, frightening yet fascinating.

People forget or do not realise how the Poles themselves have lost huge chunks of their history, and have schooled themselves not to talk about it. Wojtek, though, brings them face to face with lost realities, and that is important. For if we do not know the road we have travelled, we have no signposts to guide us into the future. When I left the president's office, I thought: another convert, Wojtek. Well done!

On Tuesday 15 November 2011, there was another development. I travelled to London for the screening of a new TV documentary: *Wojtek The Bear That Went to War*. My husband Andrew and I, our son Alexander (who was an extra in the film), our daughter Janie and her flatmate Marc MacInnes, who were runners for the film crew, all attended the preview at the Riverside Studios in Hammersmith. I was quite nervous because not only was I in the documentary, I had also been asked to be part of the discussion panel after the screening. I am usually quite confident, but with Wojtek there is always a need to get things right, and although I had great faith in the production, I had not anticipated so many people would be attending, especially those who had personally known Woj-tek. For me it was a first meeting with many of the people I had either written about or corresponded with by email. I need not have worried. It was the first time, for example, I had met Professor Wojciech Narebski, or 'Little Wojtek', as he became known. He was one of the many who travelled with Wojtek, and his recollections of him were spell-binding, as so many of these stories are, without the author having any understanding of the effect on the listener. These spontaneous and unscripted remniscences are far more powerful than slick powerpoint presentations. The documentary was superb; Will Hood and Adam Lavis directed it and Kat Mansoor and Kasia Skibinska were the producers. Ironically, the cameraman was Wojciech Staron, whom we told was put on this planet to film Wojtek! Collectively known as Animal Monday, Will, Adam and Kat were by now well-known to us; indeed, had become part of our family, as well as the family of Wojtek. To see their work come to fruition was fantastic. It was odd sitting in a theatre in London watching our farm, and indeed ourselves, on film. Even Holly, one of our pet spaniels, made the silver screen, in her usual laidback way. But the icing on the cake was the narration by Brian Blessed. His most memorable quote lives with me still: 'The story of Wojtek would make God smile.'

One of the most important contributions to the film was made by former soldier Archibald (Archie) Brown. Archie had been a mine of information and enjoyed working with the film crew. He died a few weeks later and the film was dedicated to him. When he talked about the bear, it was with deep respect and love. At the end of his contribution he broke down on screen, and we all shared his grief. Watching him, there was not a dry eye in the house. He stated what we all thought in our hearts: we had no right to forget Wojtek. He was, indeed, a treasured being whose passing was as an old soldier, not just a beloved pet.

On 23 January 2012 I received a surprise email from the UK embassy in Warsaw. It was an invitation from the UK ambassador, Robin Barnett, to be guest of honour at their Celebration of Scotland in Poland evening on 6 February. When I finally linked up with First Secretary to the ambassador, Iain Stewart, a fellow Scot who used to live in the Borders at Bowden, close to my own home. I was left in no doubt that this was a serious diplomatic initiative to promote stronger trade and cultural links between Scotland and Poland. Naturally, I jumped at the chance to take the bear to Poland for the first time.

At Heathrow, carrying Alan Herriot's maquette of Wojtek in a plastic bag, I made my way to the bus waiting to take us to Terminal Three and our flight to Warsaw. Being naturally inquisitive, the bear poked his nose out of the plastic bag and stared out. A child spotted him, raised his hand and touched the bear's nose. While in transit he chatted away in German to the bear, confidently believing the bear was his new friend. The innocence and the joy of the encounter were palpable. His parents smiled at the scene. As we parted, the child laughed and waved goodbye to Wojtek before disappearing into the huge glass departure lounge for his flight onwards to who knows where. Say what you like, the bear makes friends easily.

Security being security, Wojtek had to pass through a variety of scanners. Finally the flight was ready to leave, and just as I rose to shuffle forward for embarkation, four young Poles spotted him and shouted, 'Wojtek, Wojtek!' They waved enthusiastically and as they passed by patted him on the head. 'We love Wojtek,' said one of them. Though their English was limited, I got the message: I was not very important but my companion Wojtek enjoyed superstar status.

When I arrived in Poland it was −26°F on the streets. But I found it bracing very cold and dry, with no chilly wind. I was met by Maja Andrzejewska from the embassy. She was fascinated by Wojtek's story, as many young Poles are. For many of them it is a new tale, and they eagerly absorb the details. En route to the embassy I unwrapped Wojtek in the car and sat him on my knee so he could see Poland's capital city. Maja enjoyed the moment too, and we both laughed because in a way it was a celebration. Wojtek had come to his spiritual home.

There was a quick turnaround at the embassy so that we could be at the reception early to meet the rest of the embassy staff. On his plinth in the embassy, Wojtek looked really at home. Guests entering the reception could see him from the doorway; indeed, the glass-fronted room meant we could be seen from outside too. Staring at his poignant reflection in the glass, I felt proud that others, too, had faith in what we were doing, and I wished the moment could have been shared with so many other people who had never been able to return to Poland – with Kay Karolewski, for example, who had been with the bear in Winfield Camp all those years ago. Kay was not a sentimental man, being fairly matter of fact about his relationship with Wojtek. But he was proud to be part of the story, and I now understood why, at other functions where the bear was present, he used to stand to one side, observing people's reaction to the maquette, and quietly surging with emotion.

Others too were transfixed by Wojtek's power that night. Ambassador Robin Barnett is one of those rare people who can see into the soul, and he fully understood the message the bear was sending out. Wojtek touched people's hearts. The ambassador saw the links, and the opportunities to express these in a way which embraced both the past and the future.

After the entertainments, which included a stirring address to the haggis by Adam Chuzanow and a superb performance from the Czestochowa Pipe Band, it was my turn to 'sing for my supper' and to introduce Wojtek to the assembled crowd. I never work from set speeches so I have little remembrance of what I said. But I know I did stress that Wojtek was special for both our nations and something that linked them in a powerful way. If the Scottish soldiers respected and held in high regard the Poles who had laid down their lives for our freedom, and their freedom too, why not bring this story to Poland and let people hear about those who had lived and worked with Wojtek? His story was different because he never got to see Poland, like many who had travelled with him. Although there is great sadness in the story of Wojtek, the legacy he left is beyond normality: he was an animal who knew nothing about being a lesser species; he was, in his own mind, a soldier who had Polish as his first language; his family were Polish, and his life was as that of the men languishing in a Displaced Persons camp in Scotland waiting for a freedom that never came for so many. The core reason for doing this whole project was to bring Wojtek to Poland, along with the memory of the men, women and children who were with him from Persia to Scotland, and to tell the story of their survival. One of the most thrilling moments of the evening for me was to see for the first time the Polish edition of Wojtek's story. Publisher Mateusz Bandurski had brought along a number of copies for distribution to the guests, and for me that was a major event. It meant that for the first time Poles could read about him in their own language. They were learning something about those lost years.

On my final day it was my turn to learn as I discovered the enormity of the horror of the Warsaw Uprising on a visit to the Muzeum Powstania Warszawskiego, which manager Anna Kotonowicz had opened specially for us. The museum is a modern facility which matches anything in the UK. And it is a sombre testament to man's inhumanity to man. The Warsaw Uprising had been wholesale slaughter; the conditions for those residents for all ages, class or religion could only be described as hell on earth. In 1939 Warsaw's population was 1.9 million; by 1945 it was a mere 1,000. Anna was a highly knowledgeable guide. While walking through the museum I said to myself: 'I now understand why this project is so important to me. My grandfather must have known about this slaughter, and he had seen similar scenes in France.'

You cannot leave such an exhibition without being moved to tears. For me it was a short, three-minute film by an American pilot which brought the carnage into sharp and compelling perspective. This museum should never be missed. It is a reminder of what can happen if we fail to strive for peace. It is also quite overwhelming because the museum is sited in the area where so many innocent people were murdered. The sheer scale of the number of those deaths is difficult to comprehend. Needless to say, it took me some time to process the museum visit in my head. When you see pictures of wartime Warsaw, you understand why many Poles could not return; there was simply nothing to come back to. The city was razed to the ground, virtually all its citizens died, with no documentation to say how they met their end. There was no tangible measure of their existence save mile after mile of graves.

As the Polish soldiers sat in Winfield Camp, they had little knowledge of the true extent of the killing and destruction that had occurred in Warsaw. What they pictured in their mind's eye was the elegant capital of 1939, the Paris of Eastern Europe, with ladies in their beautifully tailored finery, welcoming restaurants, superb theatre shows, fast cars and shops filled with fine food and wines and the latest fashions. But by 1945 Hitler's hatred of the Poles had put an end to that, and many of the exiled Poles had no knowledge of the scale of the destruction which had been wrought, nor I think could they have endured the pain of knowing.

If there was no place for the men in post-war Poland, then there was certainly no place for a bear. For those who may question this, visit the museum. I had been totally unprepared for the beauty of Warsaw, although not unaware of the problems still being unravelled and worked on. It was a revelation to see a modern bustling city where workers scuttle in and out of Marks and Spencer in their lunch hour and the many cranes building more offices.

We lunched in the restored Old Town, which is very beautiful. Built from the rubble of destroyed buildings, it is a testimony to those who pieced it all together to re-create what was lost. No one should doubt its authenticity. How often have we broken a national treasure only to have it reconstructed and repaired to perfection? In rebuilding it, the joy of its existence is also restored.

For a split second, I could imagine the Winfield soldiers standing with Wojtek in the Old Town square. We watch so much on TV about the First and Second World Wars, yet we do not always absorb the true horror of these stories. When friends once told me about entering the main gate at the death camp of Auschwitz, they related their feeling of panic and a sense of oppression weighing on them as they walked through, I had no idea that fellow Europeans – people so close geographically and socially to my own – could suffer the agonies of war with no hope.

For Poles, Wojtek was one of those few beacons of hope in the history of their nation. He was a symbol of hope for the future. He could not have visited postwar Warsaw. The soldiers' dream of returning to Poland, and Warsaw, with Wojtek marching through the city to the music of bands watched by crowds of cheering children was just that – a dream. There were no streets, no marching bands and, much worse, no children. How could Wojtek have lived in the rubble with his grieving comrades? His life would have been intolerable, just as it was for millions of humans. Wojtek's transfer to a zoo in Edinburgh was not ideal, but here at least he was safe and secure. He had keepers who cared about him and a daily audience to amuse him, and sometimes visits from old friends who sang to him in Polish. And they swore he cried as he listened.

But Wojtek can now go to Poland. It won't be in the way that was originally hoped for by the men who knew him. But it will be in a much better way. His statue there will tell a new story to many, and rekindle fond memories in others.

In marked contrast to the glacial pace of so many in Scotland, the Polish reaction to the proposal of a statue to commemorate Wojtek in Warsaw was a great tonic. On returning home, phone calls and emails flooded in from people wanting to help. Most refreshing of all was the 'can do' attitude of Polish officials, who very quickly got to work compiling a shortlist of potential sites for a Wojtek statue. Indeed, their enthusiasm was so palpable it had a profound effect upon me. In Scotland I could feel my energy being drained as the project became more and more burdened with red tape. However, Polish enthusiasm was so refreshing that it quickly revived my flagging spirits. The Poles see in Wojtek an icon which straddles past and future. He is not a bear who should be left in limbo: he is a symbol of what can be achieved through friendship and trust.

I have always known that once a memorial is built in Poland, the mission, in some ways, will be complete. However, I suspect Wojtek will continue to surprise us. In life, he was an extraordinary animal with a strong sense of mischief. There is no reason to suppose his shade has lost that sense of humour. There is one continuous blessing for the rest of us: you can't be around Wojtek too long and take yourself too seriously. He also has a sneaky habit of making people do exactly what he wants. Wojtek always cajoled and charmed those who saw him. Some night have seen him as simply a wild animal, but these were few and far between. Most saw, and continue to see, him as much more – a symbol of hope, friendship, trust and freedom that, fifty years after his death, has the power to melt even the hardest of hearts.

# Epilogue

*Neal Ascherson*

What were Polish soldiers doing in Persia? Come to that, what were they doing in Scotland, both during and after the Second World War?

Aileen Orr's beautiful story is in many ways complete in itself. But to be fully appreciated, it needs to be set in its wider historical context. This background must include the disasters which fell upon Poland in the Second World War, the struggles of the Polish people to regain their freedom and the fate of those who adopted Wojtek: Poland's soldiers, sailors and airmen. These men and women had won a war which they alone had fought from its very first day to its very last, and yet they had lost their country.

Their story is one of the grandest narratives of human faith and endurance to emerge from the horrible twentieth century. It is a story still almost unknown outside Poland and the Polish-speaking diaspora scattered across the world. It explains how a very special animal, a truly remarkable individual of a bear who thought of himself as a Polish soldier, came to be so important to a very special group of men. They were tough and hardened survivors and warriors, but they had lost most of what is supposed to make a war worth fighting and a life worth living. Wojtek gave them hope, and the chance to protect, teach and care for another living being. In times of lonely despair, a bear helped them to stay human.

They had lost their families. Some utterly, because their families were no longer alive, others had lost contact with them in the chaos and terror of the Nazi and Soviet occupations. And they had lost their homes. For most of the soldiers who adopted Wojtek and fed him and played with him, their homes lay in Polish provinces newly seized and annexed by the Soviet Union. They could only return to those territories if they agreed to become Soviet citizens, and even then they would risk arrest. For others, it became clear as the war continued that 'victory' would not give Poland back its independence and freedom. Instead, their country would become – against the wishes of almost all its people – a Communist satellite state controlled by Moscow. That could not be the Poland they recognised as home, and many of them were wrestling with the realisation that they would never return to it.

So Wojtek was both a consolation and a symbol. Like the soldiers, he had no home except the army, no family except his human comrades in uniform. And yet, like them, he somehow remained an optimist, endlessly adaptable to new camps, new climates, different countries with different food, unknown languages and strange customs.

To understand more clearly why Wojtek's rugged, undaunted presence made him so much more than a mascot, that wide background of Poland at war has to be unrolled. This bear who thought that he was a soldier was also an actor in an enormous drama, as millions of men, women and children – already dispersed across Eurasia as the human debris of war – set out on a series of journeys. Some of these journeys were the long, circuitous marches of armies pursuing an enemy. Some were deportations, as whole populations were evicted and transported thousands of miles to a distant wilderness. Some began with gatherings of survivors and fugitives who then embarked on voyages across seas and deserts which were supposed one day to bring them back to Poland.

There are easy metaphors for these journeys, none of them accurate. Many Polish people think of them as a sort of sacrificial pilgrimage. That is an image drawn from the work of the national poet Adam Mickiewicz, who in the nineteenth century adopted the Messianic doctrine that Poland was the new collective Christ, destined to be sacrificed and die in order to redeem all nations. Another labelling is to speak of a Polish *Odyssey*, or sometimes an *Aeneid*. As far as encountering terrible setbacks, obstacles and monsters on the way to a goal, this comparison works. But Odysseus after years of wandering returned to find his own wife still ruling in their own house. And Aeneas eventually fulfilled his God-given destiny by founding a new Troy in a distant land. The Poles were allowed neither of these happy ends.

The roots of all this suffering reach deep into history and geography. But Poland was not always a victim nation. In the early Middle Ages, the Christian kingdom of Poland united with the pagan Grand Duchy of Lithuania to form the 'Polish–Lithuanian Commonwealth', and for several centuries the Commonwealth dominated east–central Europe. It was a strange, ramshackle structure, in many ways archaic but in other ways curiously appealing to the political ideals of our own democracy. The Commonwealth, ruled by an elected king, was multi-ethnic and in general tolerant of differences. Ethnic Poles, Ukrainians, Tatars, Ruthenians, Germans, Lithuanians, Belorussians, Armenians and Jews managed to live together, culturally distinct but united in loyalty to the Polish Crown. The diversity of faiths – Catholic Christian, Orthodox, Uniate, Lutheran and Calvinist, Islamic and Judaic

– caused no serious problems until the Counter-Reformation began to impose a dominant Catholic identity upon Poland.

And Poland became rich. From the fifteenth century on, the demand for Polish wheat to feed the rapidly-growing populations of the Netherlands, northern France and England began to make profits for Polish landowners. It was now that the Polish connection with Scotland began. From the early sixteenth century, carefully recruited groups of Scottish settlers sailed across the North Sea and the Baltic to Danzig (Gdańsk) and fanned out across the basin of the Vistula river. Along its tributaries, they founded small, tightly structured colonies which organised and financed the transport of grain down to the Baltic. Their numbers are disputed, but the Scots who joined these colonies over their two centuries of peak prosperity, most of them from the east and north-east coast of Scotland, must have been counted in the tens of thousands.

It was Scotland's first planned stride into the outside world. And yet this episode was until recently almost completely forgotten by Scottish historians – although well remembered by the Poles. Scots enjoying the Crown's protection became generals, bankers and even potentates – Alexander Chalmers from Dyce, near Aberdeen, was several times mayor of Warsaw. The traveller William Lithgow, from Lanark, who walked through Poland in the early seventeenth century, wrote that 'for auspiciousness, I may rather tearme [Poland] to be a Mother or Nurse, for the youth and younglings of Scotland who are yearly sent hither in great numbers . . . And certainly Polland may be tearmed in this kind to be the mother of our Commons and the first commencement of all our best Merchants' wealth, or at least most part of them.'

But by the early eighteenth century, the Commonwealth was growing weaker. On either flank of Poland, new and hostile states were emerging. The duchy of Muscovy expanded to become Russia of the Tsars, consolidating central power over what is now European Russia and pushing eastwards to grasp the infinite wealth of Siberia. To the west, small and backward German princedoms along the Baltic coast now merged under the new and formidable kingdom of Prussia.

The Polish Commonwealth was really a 'pre-modern' state. Central authority was weak, regional diversity was wide and political influence lay in the hands of the nobility. The new Russia and Prussia, by contrast, represented a very different and 'modern' model of power. These were grimly centralised and authoritarian states, intolerant of ethnic or religious diversity and – above all – obsessed with the training and equipping of large professional armies.

Culturally, the Polish Commonwealth considered itself more civilised than its big neighbours, whom Poles regarded as primitive. In return, the despots of Prussia and Russia loathed the relative freedom of Polish society, regarding it as a threat to their own strictly controlled systems of government. In addition, both had historical reasons to resent Poland. On the Prussian side, the Teutonic Knights had been defeated by the Poles in the fifteenth century, frustrating their drive to conquer the whole Baltic region. The Russians had suffered repeated Polish invasions and political interference in earlier centuries, in the times of Muscovy's weakness, and saw Poland as a deadly rival for control over Ukraine and Russia's western borderlands.

As the eighteenth century passed, Poland continued to decline both economically and politically. Hostile powers found that its archaic semi-democracy, with its elected monarchy and its parliament operating on a rule of unanimity, was fatally easy to corrupt and subvert. At the end of the century, Poland's neighbours used their military power to force a succession of Partitions, dividing Polish territory between Russia, Prussia and the Habsburg Empire to the south.

But after the Second Partition, Poland's last king – Stanisł aw August – and his advisers suddenly launched a dazzling programme of political and social reform, based on the principles of the American Revolution and the European Enlightenment. Poland set up the first ministry of education in Europe, and in 1791 adopted the Constitution of the Third of May, modernising the whole state structure and introducing a limited version of civil rights.

It was far too late. The Constitution enraged Catherine II, the Russian empress; she saw it as a deliberate provocation which would bring the democratic principles of the French Revolution up to her own borders. The armies tramped forward again, and the Third Partition of 1795 finally wiped what was left of Poland off the map. The eastern regions, later including Warsaw, went to Russia. The Prussian kings took what remained of western Poland, while the Habsburg Empire held southern Poland and the province of Galicia, including the city of Kraków.

There followed 123 years in which Poland did not officially exist. The three partitioning powers agreed that the very name should never be used again. Especially in the Russian area, there was a sustained effort to abolish Polish identity by suppressing the language, discriminating against the Catholic faith and criminalising those who tried to celebrate Poland's rich culture or tell the truth about its history.

This policy was an almost total failure. Polish national identity retreated into a continuous national conspiracy against the foreign occupants, which preserved culture and tradition and often erupted into armed insurrections. The first of these took place in 1795, as the Third Partition closed over the country. Led by Tadeusz Kościuszko, a Wallace-like popular hero, peasant armies won early victories until they were overwhelmed by Russian numbers. A few years later, in 1812, Napoleon promised to restore Polish independence as he invaded Russia. Tens of thousands of Poles joined his armies, fighting not only in Russia but in Austria, Italy, Spain and even in Haiti. They shed their blood in vain, but the memory of Napoleonic reforms to Poland's legal and administrative system was preserved, and revived when Poland regained its independence a century later.

In 1830, another insurrection – the November Uprising – broke out in Warsaw and rapidly spread. It took the Russians a year of hard fighting to defeat the rebels. Fierce repression followed, and almost the whole intellectual elite of Poland, most of whom had fought in or helped to organise the rising, went into exile in western Europe. The Great Emigration in effect made Paris the political capital of Poland for the next 80 years. And for the rest of the century Poland's literary and musical culture – now reaching its dazzling zenith in the work of the poets Adam Mickiewicz, Juliusz Słowacki and Cyprian Kamil Norwid, and the composer Frédéric Chopin – was almost entirely created in France.

There were other, lesser, insurrections and a network of Polish patriotic conspiracies spread over Europe. But the next full-scale rebellion – the January Uprising – did not take place until 1863. Once again, the Poles fought in their streets and in their forests, and held out for over a year. Once again, the collapse of the rising was followed by hangings and police terror, and by the familiar sight of columns of chained men and women being marched away across the snow to Siberian captivity.

But the disaster of the January Uprising led to a change of mood in Poland. There was a feeling that the time for 'romantic', sacrificial rebellions was over. Instead, Poland should concentrate on patient, 'positivist' campaigns to build up the nation's economic strength and modernise its social structures. In the Prussian partition, which after 1871 became part of a united German Empire, Polish farmers fought a long and successful struggle by legal and peaceful means to defend their land against Bismarck's policy of German colonisation.

To the east, there was a lull in the general risings against the Tsardom until the Russian Revolution of 1905, which spread throughout the Russian Empire and in Poland became simultaneously a battle for social justice and for national independence. Armed conspiracies continued to attack Tsarist officials and institutions with bomb and gun right up the outbreak of the First World War in 1914. One of these movements, the underground Polish Socialist Party, was led by a petty aristocrat from Lithuanian Poland, the charismatic plotter and soldier Józef Piłsudski.

The outbreak of the war meant that Poles in the Russian army would be fighting their Polish brothers in the German and Austro-Hungarian armies. But it also meant that the partitioning powers were fighting each other, and almost at once they began a competitive auction of offers designed to win Polish support. Russia offered semi-independence under the Tsar while Germany and Austria-Hungary attempted to set up a puppet 'Polish Kingdom' in the regions they conquered from the Russians. Piłsudski raised 'Polish Legions' in the Habsburg Empire and invaded Russian Poland; this had little effect on the war, but created a heroic legend around the legions and Piłsudski himself.

In the end, the Poles did not win back independence by their own efforts. The Polish state reappeared because of a political earthquake which transformed Eurasia and the Middle East: the collapse within a year or so of the three partition empires and the Ottoman Empire to the south. The Tsardom fell in 1917; the German and Austrian empires 18 months later. Piłsudski entered Warsaw in triumph, proclaiming the restoration of independence on 11 November 1918.

There followed several years of vicious local wars as the new Polish Republic fought to establish its frontiers in the east and west. Poland took most of the Upper Silesian industrial basin and the Poznań region from Germany, the city and district of Vilnius (Wilno) from the new Lithuanian state, and western Ukraine with the city of Lwów from Ukrainian nationalists. At the time of the Bolshevik Revolution, Lenin had allowed both Poland and Finland to take independence from Russia. But in 1920, as Polish forces reached Kiev and tried to create a Ukrainian puppet state under Polish control, the patience of the Bolsheviks ran out. The Soviet armies surged westwards, and after defeating the Poles in central Ukraine, rode on across Poland until the 'Red Cavalry' was almost on the outskirts of Warsaw.

There they were halted. Piłsudski's troops launched a counter-offensive which cut round behind the Soviet attackers and severed their communications. The Red Army fell apart, and was driven back almost to its starting-point. At the 1921 Treaty of Riga, a new eastern frontier was drawn for Poland, leaving large areas with Ukrainian or Belorussian majorities under Polish control.

The Polish–Soviet War of 1920, coming only two years after the restoration of independence, set the scene for much of what was to happen in the following decades. Although the Battle of Warsaw (the so-called 'Miracle on the Vistula') was a providential victory for Poland, the long-term consequences of the conflict were dire.

Firstly, it powerfully and permanently strengthened the ancient prejudices of both sides. The Russians were confirmed in their view that the Poles were predators and agents of

Western capitalism who had exploited Russia's weakness to seize borderlands which had always owed allegiance to Moscow. The Poles, certain that the invaders had intended to turn Poland into a Bolshevik province ruled from the Kremlin, saw the war as yet one more attempt by their traditional foe to crush Polish independence. The Bolshevik Revolution, they concluded, had merely wrapped up Russian imperial instincts in the red flag.

Secondly, grievances over the frontiers drawn at Riga were to bring disaster on the next Polish generation – the generation of soldiers who adopted Wojtek. Their homes and their families lay mostly in these borderlands. But the eastern frontiers were a compromise which satisfied neither side. Piłsudski had dreamed of a vast confederation, rather like the old Commonwealth, which would include Poland, Ukraine, Belorussia and Lithuania. In the event, he got a mainly Polish state with large and often discontented ethnic minorities: only 69 per cent of its population was Polish, while Ukrainians and other minorities outnumbered ethnic Poles in the rural parts of Western Ukraine and Western Belorussia. Between the wars, Warsaw government policy towards the minorities was often brutal, and Ukrainian nationalist organisations fought back with bombs and political assassinations.

Józef Piłsudski was the dominant figure in independent Poland until his death in 1935. Always impatient with parliamentary democracy, he retired after a few years but in 1926 returned to lead a military coup which installed an authoritarian regime. After his death, power passed into the hands of army officers with extreme right-wing opinions (the so-called 'Sanacja'). Political opposition was suppressed, left-wingers found themselves in detention camps and in the late 1930s the regime allowed itself to be pushed into racial discrimination against Jews. In foreign policy, the Sanacja pursued Piłsudski's principle of balance between Nazi Germany and Stalin's Soviet Union, favouring neither dictatorship against the other but building up Poland's independent military strength to deter German or Russian invasion.

This was an illusion. The third fateful consequence of the Polish–Soviet war was an unreal overestimate of Poland's military potential, coupled with an equally unreal faith in the infallible judgement of the army's commanders. The 1920 victory over the Red Army had been brilliant, but military technology soon moved on. The Polish army was large in numbers – it could mobilise a million men – and high in morale. But its equipment with tanks, anti-tank artillery and aircraft fell far behind the pace of rearmament in the USSR and above all in Nazi Germany. The efficiency of the Polish navy and the code-breaking skills of Polish military intelligence could not compensate for the weaknesses of the army in the field.

But the 'Second Republic' could also show some astonishing achievements. In the century and a quarter of partition, the three segments of Poland had grown apart; legal systems, education, military training, even railway gauges now had to be unified. After 1918, ambitious central planning rapidly gave Poland the outlines of an effective infrastructure and reorganised its industrial base. The new port of Gdynia was planted at the end of the 'Polish Corridor', Poland's narrow foothold on the Baltic Sea, a city complete with docks and shipyards which sprang up in a few years on the site of a fishing village. But in spite of these successes, Poland remained a strikingly backward and underdeveloped country when compared to its western neighbours. Three out of four Poles lived in the countryside, almost all of them poor peasants. Illiteracy was widespread, and rural overpopulation was recognised as the cause of shocking poverty; a plague for which the Second Republic was given no time to find a cure.

In spite of the 'non-alignment' policy, many Poles realised in the 1930s that a German attack was almost inevitable sooner or later. They also saw that non-alignment, by irritating both of Poland's dangerous neighbours and conciliating neither of them, threatened to bring about the ultimate national nightmare: an agreement between Russia and Germany to join forces and destroy Poland.

This had already happened several times in history. It was the story of the eighteenth century partitions, while at the 1812 Convention of Tauroggen, Prussian generals had agreed with the Russians to form an alliance and turn their weapons against Napoleon and his Polish supporters. Now, on the eve of war in August 1939, this lethal pattern was repeated. Nazi Germany and the Soviet Union staggered the world by suddenly overcoming their ideological enmity and signing the infamous Molotov–Ribbentrop Pact. The Poles did not then know that a secret protocol to the pact had arranged for a Fourth Partition between Russia and Germany and the abolition of Polish independence. But all their instincts about this new alliance told them to expect the worst.

Piłsudski had made a non-aggression agreement with the Soviet Union in 1932, and a similar pact with Nazi Germany in 1934. Neither Stalin nor Hitler had the slightest intention of respecting these pieces of paper. As tensions increased, the government in Warsaw made itself believe that if Germany attacked Poland, France would come to the rescue with effective military support. It was true that a French military mission led by General Weygand (and including a spindly young officer named Charles de Gaulle) had come to Warsaw and given significant help and advice during the Polish–Soviet war of 1920. But French forces, though large in numbers and well equipped with tanks, were in no condition to defend their own country in the late 1930s, let alone to fight their way across Europe to rescue a distant ally.

As Hitler crushed Czechoslovakia in 1938 and early 1939, it was obvious that his next target would be Poland. Germany had never accepted the loss of territories to Poland after the First World War. Now Hitler concentrated his threats on the Baltic port of Danzig (Gdańsk), which the 1919 Versailles Treaty had redefined as an independent 'free city', and on the 'Polish Corridor' (another Versailles invention) which separated the main Reich territory from the German territory of East Prussia.

Hitler's carefully planned onslaught began in the early hours of 1 September 1939, as the German battleship *Schleswig-Holstein* opened fire on the Polish forts at Danzig. At the same time, the Luftwaffe bombed Polish cities and the German army drove across the frontier at a dozen points.

The Second World War had begun. In some ways, the Polish forces were prepared for it. Months earlier, Polish intelligence – which had broken the German Enigma military code – had passed its secrets and an Enigma machine to the British, a gift which was to prove infinitely valuable to the Allied cause. And two days before war broke out, the Polish destroyer flotilla slipped out of Gdynia and made its way to Scotland to join the Royal Navy – another long-planned move.

But there was no way that the Poles could hold the overwhelming weight of the German attack. Against 2,600 German tanks they had only 150, and only 400 modern aircraft to send up against the Luftwaffe's 2,000 bombers and fighters. And they were facing a new kind of war: the 'blitzkrieg' use of fast-moving armoured divisions which punched through defensive lines and circled round to out-flank the enemy, while dive-bombers destroyed transport and communications and drove thousands of fleeing civilians out to block the roads.

Given their weaknesses, the Poles put up noble resistance during the September Campaign. The tales of Polish lancers charging German tanks are mostly fantasy (though there were a few such incidents), but the Germans suffered over 50,000 casualties – more than the British and French together inflicted on them in France the following year. The Germans had not expected such a stubborn defence, and were dismayed when a counter-attack on the Bzura river temporarily threw them back and caused them heavy losses. But the Poles had a strategy problem as well as an equipment problem.

In 1939, both France and Britain had promised to declare war on Germany if Poland were invaded, and they duly did so on 3 September. There had also been military talks that summer, which the Poles had understood to mean that in the event of war France would attack Germany across the Rhine with full force. The Polish task was therefore to hold up the German armies for about two weeks to allow the French offensive to succeed. But nothing of the kind happened. There was no French offensive, and no military, air or naval assistance was sent to Poland from either France or Britain. This was the first of Poland's many bitter disappointments with the Western Allies.

Warsaw was soon surrounded, although the government managed to escape to the south-east. The Polish armies were in retreat, but still fighting hard, when on 17 September the Red Army crossed the frontier without warning and attacked them from behind.

Moscow announced that Poland had ceased to exist, and that its eastern provinces of Western Ukraine and Western Belorussia were being taken over by the Soviet Union to protect their inhabitants. Caught between two enemies, the

Polish forces fell apart and organised resistance ceased. Many thousands of prisoners of war were rounded up by the Red Army, and transported eastwards to unknown destinations in the Soviet Union.

From this awful moment in late September 1939, three diverging paths led into the future for Poland's soldiers. On one point, however, everyone was united. Poland, unlike France or Belgium or several other nations conquered by Hitler, would not surrender. Józef Piłsudski had written that 'to be defeated, but not to give in, is victory!' Somehow, somewhere, the war to restore an independent Poland had to go on.

The first of the three paths led across Europe to France and Britain. The second path led back into occupied Poland itself, into the armed resistance movements which at once began to spring up. The third path began in the prison camps and convict settlements of the Soviet Union, and traversed vast distances to cross Iran, Iraq, Palestine and Egypt before reaching Italy. It was along this third journey, the longest and most arduous of them all, that Polish soldiers found and adopted a bear cub they named Wojtek.

All these paths had branches, potholes and forks. All those who travelled on them hoped that they would finally converge in a liberated and democratic Poland. But most of them did not live to see their grandchildren reach the end of those roads. Poland did not regain full independence and democracy until 1989.

The first path began at a bridge, which crossed a shallow frontier river called the Czeremosz. For a week or so after 17 September, the Soviet forces did not seal off the borders in Poland's south-eastern corner, allowing the army commanders and the president to cross into Romania followed by tens of thousands of officers and soldiers. Many others escaped over the southern mountains into Hungary. A third group headed north into Lithuania, then still precariously independent, and was interned after surrendering.

On 30 September, a new government-in-exile was set up by General Władysław Sikorski, who became both prime minister and commander-in-chief. Based in Paris, this government was in many ways a coup against the old Sanacja regime carried out by Sikorski, a famous officer who had gone abroad in the 1930s in order to form a centre of opposition to the ageing Piłsudski and his successors. Even before Sikorski took over, officers and men were escaping from Romanian internment and heading west to rejoin the war. One group of soldiers from Romania and Hungary managed to find a ship to Syria, where they joined French forces as the 'Carpathian Rifle Brigade'. But the bulk of the troops who had escaped the Nazi and Soviet armies were transported to France. There they were joined by volunteers of Polish origin from all over western Europe to form a force which eventually numbered some 80,000 men.

Early in 1940, troops from Sikorski's army in France went into action with British and French forces during the inconclusive Norway campaign. When the main German offensive burst into France that May, the Poles fought skilfully, but they were driven back and separated by the rapid onrush of the Panzer divisions and by the collapse of French units on their flanks.

France surrendered on 22 June 1940. Sikorski had already moved to London with the exile government, and some 23,000 of his troops – most of them evacuated from the ports of northern and western France – managed to reach Britain. Several thousand naval and air force personnel were already there, including the Polish pilots who were to play a decisive part that summer with the Royal Air Force in the Battle of Britain. But the Poles had to leave three-quarters of their men behind. Most of them became prisoners of war, or crossed into neutral Switzerland, preferring Swiss internment to German captivity. Other Poles made their way across Spain to Portugal, hoping to travel on to Britain. Others again went underground in France itself, and later joined the French resistance.

In Britain, now facing imminent German invasion, Churchill and Sikorski agreed that the Polish army from France should be sent to Scotland. There it could re-arm and retrain with British weapons and equipment, and at the same time guard the Scottish east coast against a German landing. The first tented camps were set up between Edinburgh and Glasgow, near Biggar, Crawford and Douglas. Later, more solid accommodation was found or built for the Polish forces, as their main concentration shifted to Fife, Angus and Perthshire. General Marian Kukiel, the officer commanding this 1st Polish Corps in Scotland, set up his headquarters at Bridge of Earn. It should be added that one of Sikorski's first acts in Scotland was to set up a detention camp for his political enemies, mostly old Sanacja officers who were trying to undermine his authority. This camp was near Rothesay on the Isle of Bute, known to apprehensive Poles as the 'Isle of Snakes'.

It was to be a long time before these troops were called into action. But they trained hard, once they had overcome the gloom of their second defeat, and they were made welcome. A Scottish–Polish Society appeared, organising hospitality and entertainment, while the lord provosts of Glasgow and Edinburgh – especially Sir Patrick Dollan ('Dolanski') from Glasgow – raised funds and held supportive rallies for the Poles. A variety of special university courses were set up for the Poles, and a Polish School of Medicine at Edinburgh University awarded degrees throughout the war.

In small-town and rural Scotland, their exotic uniforms, the strange language and the outgoing charm of the ordinary soldiers made a lasting impression on communities which had never had much contact with foreigners before. Young women, unused to men who kissed their hands and danced like Fred Astaire, were especially taken with the Poles. This often led to complications, not least religious misunderstandings as a Catholic soldiery sought love and friendship in a Presbyterian countryside, But over 2,500 Scottish women married Polish soldiers during the five-year stay of the 1st Corps.

As time passed, the 1st Corps grew in numbers. A few thousand Polish soldiers were able to escape from occupied Europe, mostly though Spain, Portugal or North Africa. Later, beginning in 1942, about 7,000 men and some women arrived in Scotland from Palestine and Egypt, a small fraction of those who had escaped from Soviet captivity through Iran. (Their main body remained in the Middle East, to form what was to become the 2nd Polish Corps commanded by General Władysław Anders.) A new source of recruits opened after the Normandy landings in June 1944, as ethnic Poles unwillingly conscripted into the German armies surrendered and – after screening – volunteered to join the Polish forces. Some 33,000 of these '*Wehrmacht* Poles' reached Scotland in the course of 1944, followed by another 15,000 up to the end of the war.

By now, though, other Polish troops were leaving Scotland and going into action in northern Europe. Two new formations had been trained up and equipped. One was the Polish Parachute Brigade under General Stanisław Sosabowski, which did most of its training in Fife around Leven and Largo.

Sikorski's original idea, and the inspiration for the Brigade's morale, had been to drop the parachutists into Poland itself, to achieve the nation's liberation as an advance-guard of the Western Allies.

But as the Soviet armies began to approach the Polish frontiers, long before the British and Americans could open a second front in France, it became obvious that Poland would be liberated by the Red Army alone, and the plan to send the Brigade into Poland was shelved. In August 1944, during the doomed Warsaw Rising, the British turned down desperate but impractical Polish appeals to let the Brigade join the insurgents. It was not until the next month that Sosabowski's men finally went into battle, as part of the disastrous Allied attempt to seize the Rhine bridges at Arnhem by mass parachute landings.

The other formation created in Scotland was the 1st Polish Armoured Division. Led by the legendary General Stanisław Maczek, it numbered about 15,000 men. Maczek embodied Polish military history in his own person. By the time that his division landed in Normandy in July 1944, he had fought in the First World War (in the Habsburg army), in the defence of Lwów against the Ukrainians in 1918–19, in the Polish– Soviet war of 1920, in the September campaign of 1939 in Poland, and in France in 1940.

At the climax of the Normandy fighting, the Polish tanks were sent to close the Falaise Gap, the exit from a pocket in which two German armies with several Panzer divisions had been encircled. Maczek's men, heavily outnumbered, took the full force of the German armour trying to escape. The Poles held on, and Falaise turned into the bloodiest defeat the *Wehrmacht* experienced at the hands of the Western Allies. Later, the 1st Armoured Division drove eastwards across France and into the Low Countries. The Poles are still joyfully

remembered for liberating the Dutch city of Breda, and streets
are named after General Maczek there and in Antwerp.

At the end of the war, the division fought its way into
northern Germany. But after the Nazi surrender, both the 1st
Armoured Division and the Parachute Brigade (which had
also entered Germany in early 1945) took on a new role: the
rescue of the enormous mass of Poles who had landed up in
Germany as slave workers, concentration camp prisoners,
prisoners of war and even children removed from their parents
by the Nazis for 'Germanisation'. Hundreds of thousands of
penniless, emaciated human beings were now on the roads,
seeking food, shelter and repatriation. To help them, the
Polish Army took a bold step. With British permission, they
took over the town of Haren, expelled all its German
inhabitants, renamed it 'Maczków' in their general's honour
and converted it into a huge reception centre for displaced
Poles.

The second path back to a free Poland lay through resistance
within Poland itself. This meant almost exclusively resistance
to the German occupation. The massive deportations of the
Polish population from the eastern borderlands annexed by
the Soviet Union made partisan warfare there almost impossible to organise. In any case, the Nazi invasion in June
1941 transformed the Soviet Union from enemy into 'gallant
ally'.

As the September campaign ended in 1939, Polish units –
cavalry as well as infantry – were already taking to the forests
and mountains. In cities and towns, centres of patriotic
conspiracy sprang up. Poland had been defeated but had
not surrendered, and there were to be almost no collaborators
with the Nazi occupation. As the historian Norman Davies
has put it, 'there was never any Polish Quisling, for the simple

reason that in Poland the Nazis never really tried to recruit one.' Their long-term plan for the Poles was to enslave and ultimately to exterminate them, not to enlist them as allies. This gave the Poles a simple moral choice: to fight or to be obliterated.

By November 1939, Sikorski in France was in contact with many of these resistance groups, drawing them together into a coherent command structure answering to the government-in-exile. The movement eventually took the name of *Armia Krajowa* (Home Army) or 'AK' for short. After Hitler's attack on the Soviet Union, a separate, militant but much smaller Communist resistance appeared, the 'People's Guard' or 'People's Army' (AL). But its relations with the AK were wary, and it took orders from the underground Communist leadership rather than from Sikorski's government in London.

As German repression and deportations for forced labour grew more intense, the AK was joined by 'peasant battalions' raised from the countryside. By 1943, it had become the biggest resistance movement in the whole of Nazi-occupied Europe, eventually numbering over 400,000 men and wo-men. But the AK itself was only the military wing of a complete underground state, equipped with a *Delegatura* representing the exile government, with 'councils' drawn from the main political parties, and with most of the apparatus of a normal country down to a chain of clandestine uni-versities and a vigorous illegal press.

For the London government-in-exile, keeping in touch with the AK and its affiliates was difficult; dangerous but crucial. In Scotland, at training centres at Polmont and Largo or at the Polish 'spy school' in Glasgow, agents were trained as parachutists and radio operators and dropped back into Poland from long-range aircraft. Many were lost, but gradually regular and reliable radio communication between the *Dele-*

*gatura*, the AK command and the London government was established. Even riskier was the return journey of couriers from Poland, sometimes smuggled on neutral ships through Scandinavia, sometimes – later in the war – picked up by Allied light aircraft from secret airstrips. (In July 1944, the AK used one of these flights to deliver to the British the working parts and guidance system of a prototype V-2 rocket, stolen from a Nazi missile range.)

The couriers who reached London did not only bring despatches from the resistance. They were themselves direct witnesses to the appalling nature of the Nazi occupation. The messenger Jan Karski laid before British and American statesmen the full news of the Jewish genocide. Jan Nowak (Jeziorański) was sent out of burning Warsaw during the 1944 uprising to plead with the Allies for help. In the West, most people knew that the occupation was brutal, especially in its treatment of the Jews. But the governments of the democracies were slow, even reluctant, to believe the sheer scale and intensity of horror which the Polish messengers and the exile government revealed to them.

In German-occupied Poland, some 5.4 million people died in concentration camps or mass executions, 3 million of them Jews. That figure does not include casualties caused directly by war and, in all, Poland lost roughly a fifth of its pre-war population. Its industry and infrastructure were almost completely destroyed, while much of Poland's cultural heritage was burned or looted. In 1944, the whole central city of Warsaw was blown up on Hitler's orders and reduced to rubble.

After the 1939 invasion, the Nazis divided their half of Poland into two regions. The first consisted of territory in the west of the country which was simply absorbed into the Reich, the Polish population being driven out and replaced by German settlers. The second region was the 'General

Government', a kind of colonial protectorate ruled from Kraków by the tyrannical Hans Frank. It was in the General Government that almost all the extermination camps were constructed for the Jewish Holocaust, the industrial murder of Europe's Jews by gas. (Auschwitz lay just outwith the General Government, in the Upper Silesian region absorbed by the Reich.)

In the General Government, the SS began a programme of selective genocide, designed to destroy the Polish elite and to prevent any national revival. Academics, creative intellectuals and the priesthood were targeted. A little later, the German authorities started to round up the first of 3.5 million men and women for slave labour in German war industries or agriculture. Villages which resisted were burned down; their men were shot, the women deported and the children either killed or kidnapped for 'Germanisation' in German families.

These conditions brought immense popular support for the resistance. But at first the AK concentrated on building up its strength and acquiring weapons, and it was not until 1942 that widespread attacks on the German occupiers began. The price for resistance, even for disobeying regulations, was usually death. In the cities, the Germans carried out random mass round-ups of 'hostages' who were lined up against walls and shot, their bodies left lying on the street as a warning against defiance or disobedience. Ghettos were set up in the towns, as a prelude to the Jewish genocide, and the penalty for hiding an escaped Jew was immediate execution for the rescuer and his or her whole family.

In spite of these risks, the underground state survived and proliferated. This was not a new idea. During and after the January rising of 1863, the insurgents had established a 'parallel nation' which preserved Polish identity through illegal publishing, education and even clandestine courts. The AK's arms and explosives were captured from the Germans, and later parachuted in from the West. But the resistance was able to do little to help the Warsaw Ghetto Rising in April 1943, as Jewish fighters decided to die fighting rather than go passively to the gas chambers of Treblinka.

By the end of 1943, AK partisan units were in control of many districts of rural Poland, especially the forests and hills of the old eastern borderlands which now lay behind German lines. But once again, strategic problems emerged. In 1943, the plan of the government-in-exile and the AK command inside Poland had been to harry the Germans as they retreated and then to join the Soviet armies as they drove the *Wehrmacht* out of Poland. But early in 1944, as Soviet troops advanced across the pre-war Polish frontiers, it became clear that the Russians had no intention of restoring Polish authority in the regions they had seized in 1939.

Worse still, they treated the AK units which welcomed them as potential enemies. The Polish partisans were offered a choice between arrest and conscription into the Red Army. Places liberated by the Home Army were handed over to the People's Army, the Communist partisans, and to their Committee for National Liberation (PKWN). This body had been set up in Moscow as the nucleus for a future Communist government of Poland.

For the London government and the AK command, the outlook in the spring of 1944 was grim. It was now obvious that Stalin intended to set up a puppet Communist regime in Poland, or at least a government which took its orders from Moscow. He would ignore the legal government-in-exile, and suppress its armed forces. As the Soviet armies blasted their way through the Nazi defences in eastern Poland and headed towards Warsaw, Polish leaders adopted a new and desperate plan of action.

Operation Tempest was meant to be an all-out general uprising in the path of the Red Army. In one district after another, the retreating Germans would be overcome and the Soviet generals would arrive to find a region of Poland already liberated and under the control of the London government. Unfortunately, Tempest was an almost complete failure. The Polish partisans fought valiantly and often drove the Germans out, but the Soviet forces were under orders to suppress them. In their moment of victory, the AK battalions were rounded up, disarmed and interned. The Polish officials they had appointed in the liberated areas were arrested.

In late July 1944, Soviet tank patrols were seen in the Warsaw outskirts, on the far bank of the Vistula. At the same time, German civilians and officials in Warsaw began to evacuate the city. General Tadeusz Bór-Komorowski, in command of the AK, now took a snap decision to order a general urban insurrection. His hope was to liberate Warsaw, so that the Soviet allies would enter the free capital of Poland already under the authority of the legitimate government-in-exile.

What followed was one of the greatest tragedies in Polish history. The Warsaw Rising, almost the last of the mighty street insurrections of European history, began on 1 August 1944 and held out against overwhelming odds until 2 October. Home Army and People's Army soldiers fought side by side at the barricades. So did the civilian population. Small boys ran to fling grenades at tanks. Schoolgirls running with despatches under fire died by the hundred. By the time that Warsaw surrendered and the survivors had been marched out to prison camps, some 250,000 people were dead and almost the entire city was reduced to blackened ruins.

The memory of the rising later became a towering shrine of national self-sacrifice and comradeship, of martyrdom and

betrayal. At the same time, it radically and perhaps permanently changed Polish attitudes away from the Romantic
tradition of revolutionary nationalism. Another rising like
that, the survivors felt, and there would be no Poland left
to die for.

Some historians have blamed Bór-Komorowski for giving
the order to fight. But others say that the excitement in
Warsaw had reached such a pitch that fighting would have
broken out within hours anyway. There were several reasons
why the rising failed. One was that the German civilian
evacuation of Warsaw was misleading; powerful armoured
units were already moving up to the city. Another reason,
the decisive factor, was Stalin's refusal to cross the Vistula and
rescue the insurgents. The Soviet divisions which reached
the river were ordered to halt on the further bank, in full
view of burning Warsaw, and – with the exception of some
Polish units under Soviet command – made no attempt to
cross. Stalin knew precisely what was in Bór-Komorowski's
mind, and he was content to let the Germans do his dirty
work for him. It was months after the Germans had crushed
the rising that Soviet forces crossed the river and resumed
their advance. By then Warsaw was a ghost city of unin-
habited ruins.

The Polish troops in Scotland, Italy and Normandy, like
Poles all over the world, watched in agony as Warsaw fought
and died. But there was little they could do. Some long-range
aircraft, Polish, British and South African, managed to reach
Warsaw from airfields in Italy, but they suffered terrible losses
and the supplies and ammunition they dropped often fell into
German hands. Predictably, Stalin refused to let the Allies use
airfields in Soviet-held territory until it was too late. The
British, for their part, refused to let the London Poles fly the
Parachute Brigade to Warsaw.

From the military point of view, that would have been suicidal madness. But there was political reluctance too. Both Churchill and Roosevelt knew that the Soviet Union was carrying the main burden of a war now approaching its climax. They were determined not to let 'Polish problems' disturb their partnership with Stalin.

After the collapse of the rising, the Home Army in the rest of Poland began to disintegrate. A few groups retreated into the forests and carried on a hopeless guerrilla war against the new Communist authorities. Within a few years, anyone who had fought in the Home Army fell under suspicion as a 'counter-revolutionary', and thousands were imprisoned. The parachute couriers from Scotland were hunted down by Soviet military intelligence, and some – caught with their radios tuned to the Polish government in London – were tried and shot as 'imperialist spies'. The true story of the Warsaw Rising, and the main role in the resistance played by the non-Communist Home Army, became forbidden topics.

From trenches in Italy, or from camps in Lowland Scotland, Wojtek's friends watched this process in deepening despair. Although they did not know it, their country had already been abandoned by Britain and America. At the Teheran summit in late 1943, Stalin, Roosevelt and Churchill had agreed that Poland should remain under Soviet occupation when it was liberated and that the new eastern frontier established by the Soviet invasion in 1939, leaving the cities of Lwów and Wilno (Vilnius) in Soviet hands, should become permanent. As compensation, Poland would be given the eastern provinces of Germany. The whole country would be shifted 150 miles to the west.

The Yalta conference in February 1945 did little more than publicly confirm these decisions. Postwar Europe would be divided into 'spheres of influence' – with Poland left in the

Soviet sphere. Roosevelt and Churchill eagerly accepted
Stalin's assurance that there would be free elections in Poland.

It didn't escape the soldiers' notice that Poland was invited
to neither of these meetings, nor to the Big Three Potsdam
Conference after the Nazi surrender. It was behind closed
doors that the 'Victor Powers' had dictated Poland's political
future.

General Sikorski had died in a plane crash at Gibraltar in
1943. His successor as prime minister in the London government was Stanisław Mikołajczyk, a peasant politician who
tried desperately but vainly to save what he could from the
Yalta settlement. But the Communist-led Committee of
National Liberation had now become the provisional government of Poland. In July 1945, a few months after Germany's
unconditional surrender, Britain and the United States with-
drew recognition from the London government-in-exile and
transferred it to the Communist-led regime in Warsaw.

At first, the new regime pretended to be an alliance of
'progressive forces' and Mikołajczyk felt able to join a coalition government in Warsaw. But the Communists controlled
the security police and within two years the opposition was
being crushed by violence and threats. The promised free
elections produced crudely faked results. Late in 1947, Mikoł
ajczyk fled Poland, hidden in the back of an American
diplomatic car. The Communist monopoly of power soon
became complete.

By now, Poland was being ruled by state terror. Veterans of
the AK were still being rounded up and imprisoned. The
Home Army commanders were kidnapped, taken to Moscow
and tried on incredible charges such as 'collaborating with the
Nazis'. Returning soldiers who had served in the Polish armies
under British command were treated as suspected traitors and
saboteurs.

The Polish troops in the West, by now demobilised and living in temporary camps scattered over England and Scotland, knew what was going on. The postwar British government hoped that they would go back to Poland, but – in a rare act of guilt-driven generosity – promised to care for them if they preferred to stay.

It was a miserable choice that they all faced. Most of them longed to go home and help rebuild their beloved, shattered land. But there they would be rewarded by persecution, by the sadness of life under foreign tyranny. On the other hand, what future could they have in a land whose language they hardly spoke, where they lacked friends, where their skills beyond manual labour and soldiering seemed to count for nothing?

But for the men who lived with Wojtek in the camp at Winfield, the choice was a little easier. Before they came across that bear cub in the Persian hills, they had seen the real face of Soviet Communism and had experienced on their own bodies its brutality, its callous indifference to human suffering, its hunger and its lies. If Poland were to become like that, it would no longer be a country they could live in. These were the men who had travelled the third path, and they knew only too well what they were being offered.

The third path, like the first, began on 17 September 1939, in south-eastern Poland. But this path led eastwards, into the depths of the Soviet Union. A part of the defeated Polish army was able to escape over the border into Romania and Hungary. But some 200,000 others were captured by the Soviet invaders and became prisoners of war. Some 15,000 of them, mostly officers, were moved into three prison camps in Russia and Ukraine: Kozielsk, Starobielsk and Ostaszków.

All over the regions which had been Poland's eastern provinces, Poles in responsible jobs – teachers, judges, police chiefs, mayors, editors – were arrested and imprisoned. Under directions from Moscow, the local Communist Parties in what was now Western Belorussia and Western Ukraine filled the posts with their own Belorussian or Ukrainian supporters.

But this turned out to be only the first act in an immense programme designed to obliterate Polish identity for ever in this part of eastern Europe. In February 1940, the Soviet authorities began the first mass expulsion of the Polish civilian population. Troops from the NKVD (predecessor of the KGB, as the political security force) herded Polish families to railway stations and crammed them into unheated cattle wagons. From there, the trains set forth on journeys which could last many weeks, and which the old, the youngest children and the sick often did not survive, until the prisoners were dumped in Arctic labour camps, at railheads near Siberian mines or on the empty steppes of Kazakhstan.

More deportations followed in 1940, until by early 1941 something like 1.5 million Poles – Christians and Jews, Communists and Catholics – had been driven into exile. For the gulag empire, the life or death of these slave labourers was a matter of indifference. By the time that they were allowed to leave the camps, in the summer of 1941, between a third and a half of the deported Poles were dead from hunger, exposure, exhaustion and disease.

As Aileen Orr makes clear, this had been the experience of Wojtek's companions in Scotland. Their homes before the war had been in eastern Poland. They, and often enough their families, had been among those deported to Siberia and central Asia. Somehow, they had survived. But Siberia was to be only a halting-place along the third path.

On 22 June 1941, the history of the world changed. That morning Hitler launched Operation Barbarossa, the invasion of the Soviet Union. With that order, Hitler set in motion a chain of consequences which were to shape the lives of hundreds of millions of people for the next half-century.

In the longest term, Hitler created postwar Europe. On that day, he began a war which could only end in his defeat. That defeat, in turn, would inevitably bring about the destruction of Germany, the arrival of Russian power in the centre of the continent and the partition of Europe into two hostile military camps. In this way, the Cold War – lasting roughly 42 years – was Adolf Hitler's legacy to those who survived him, and to their children and grandchildren.

The medium-term consequence was a reversal of alliances. The Soviet Union, until yesterday Hitler's accomplice in the destruction of Poland, now became an enemy of Nazi Germany and therefore the ally of Britain. Winston Churchill at once offered Stalin support. This put the Polish exile government in a painful position, but Sikorski decided he had to follow Churchill. In July, the Soviet and Polish governments signed an agreement which granted an 'amnesty' to all Poles held in Soviet captivity, and allowed a free Polish army to be formed in the USSR to fight the Germans alongside the Red Army. The Nazi–Soviet Pact was declared null and void. But – ominously – there was no clear Soviet consent to restore Poland's pre-war frontiers.

The short-term result was to save the lives of hundreds of thousands of Polish captives. This was probably Sikorski's main motive for the agreement. In London, a section of the exile government tried in vain to unseat him; they were outraged by the word 'amnesty' (what crimes were the Poles supposed to have committed?) and deeply alarmed about the failure to get a Soviet guarantee of the pre-war borders. But the need to save the prisoners overshadowed everything.

The gulag gates were opened. Very slowly – in many

remote *lagers* and penal settlements, the camp commandants did not inform the Polish prisoners about their freedom for months – the captives emerged and set out to find the places where the Polish army was setting up its tents and huts. For some, it was a chance to become soldiers and fight again. For others, especially the civilian families, the army offered their only chance to find food, shelter and medicine. Their physical condition was shocking. Thousands died on the long, arduous journey towards the first Polish bases at Totsk and Buzuluk in the Volga steppe, and thousands more who made it to the bases were too weak and ill to survive.

The commander of this army of walking skeletons was General Władysław Anders. Still pallid after months in the NKVD's Lubianka prison, Anders told his officers that 'it is our duty to forget the past' and to fight the common Nazi enemy 'shoulder to shoulder with the Red Army'. This proved easier said than done. Stalin remained suspicious of this foreign army on Soviet soil, and the equipment and rations provided by the Soviet authorities were completely inadequate for the tens of thousands of men, women and children arriving at the bases and begging for rescue.

In addition, there was a puzzling lack of officers. Some 15,000 prisoners of war, most of them officers, could not be found. They had apparently left the three camps of Kozielsk, Starobielsk and Ostaszków, but in spite of repeated Polish pleas to Stalin, the Soviet authorities seemed not to know where the missing officers had gone. Polish emissaries travelled about the Soviet Union but could find no trace of them.

Sikorski, Anders and their colleagues began to suspect the worst. But it was only much later, when in 1943 the Germans found and excavated a mass grave in Katyń Forest near Smolensk that the truth began to emerge. The dead had all been shot, hands wired behind their back and then a bullet in the head, between April and May 1940. And the Katyn grave, containing some 5,000 corpses, turned out to be only one of many. Secret Kremlin documents, which finally came to light after the fall of the Soviet Union in 1991, revealed that the killing of the 15,000 had been part of a monstrous selective genocide of Polish elites – military, judicial, administrative – ordered by Stalin personally in early March 1940.

Meanwhile, the conditions in which the 'Anders Army' lived were becoming unbearable. The original plan had been for a Polish division to fight alongside the Red Army on the Russian front. But as the Soviet authorities cut rations and demanded a reduction in the army's numbers, Anders concluded that the only chance for his men and the civilian mass huddled around them was to get out of the Soviet Union as soon as possible.

This was a hard decision. Crowds of starving, ragged Poles were still reaching the army in its new quarters near Tashkent in Uzbekistan, and evacuation would abandon thousands of other refugees to their fate. Sikorski was at first against the idea, but on political grounds. He hoped that a free Polish army fighting alongside the Russians would give him leverage on Soviet policies when the armies reached Poland. But Anders, anxious about the state of his men and more mistrustful of Russian intentions, knew that this plan was unrealistic. Stalin, who saw all too clearly what Sikorski had in mind, agreed with Anders and allowed these troublesome aliens to leave.

The first contingent of Poles made their way down to the Caspian Sea in spring 1942. About 44,000 men and women, three-quarters of them soldiers, embarked on old steamers and were taken across to the Iranian shore of the Caspian at the port of Pahlevi, where British military teams were waiting for them with ambulances, food and medicine. In the next few months, another 70,000 were evacuated to Iran, a third of them civilians. Among them was a quiet non-commissioned officer named Lance-Corporal Peter Prendys – the man who was soon to adopt a Persian bear cub.

There are different figures for how many Poles were left behind. Some put it as high as a million. The Soviet authorities now blocked their movement south across the country, but small parties of Poles, men, women and surviving children, continued to journey towards the deserts of Turkmenistan and the mountains which marked the Persian frontier. Some of them travelled all the way on foot. A Polish mission left at Ashkhabad, on the Soviet side of the frontier, sheltered them and helped them to cross over to the city of Meshed, on the Iranian side.

At about this point, the 'third path' of the Polish soldiers forked into two branches. The Anders Army left the USSR for Iran in 1942. Out of the thousands of Poles who remained behind, a new army was formed – this time under Soviet control. Its politics were set by a small group of Polish Communists in Moscow. But the gibe that this was a 'Red Polish Army' was not the full truth. Most of its officers and men were deportees who had survived the gulag and who joined the new force simply because they had not managed to reach the Anders Army in time. They were determined to fight for their country, even under Soviet orders. Apart from the Stalin-worshipping propaganda they had to endure, the men of what became the 1st Polish Army were allowed traditional patriotic symbols and could attend Catholic Mass.

Their commander was the enigmatic General Zygmunt Berling. A conservative officer who had fought the Bolsheviks in 1920, Berling never forgave the army for censuring his conduct during a messy divorce. He was captured by Soviet forces in 1939, and for obscure reasons agreed while still in a prison camp to collaborate with the NKVD. This was not at first known to General Anders, who gave him a senior job organising the evacuation to Persia. It was only when Berling refused to leave Russia and began to organise the new army that Anders accused him of treachery, and in 1943 a Polish court-martial sentenced Berling *in absentia* to death for desertion and for assisting the (Soviet) enemy.

In reality, Berling seems to have been a cynical maverick who took this course more out of dislike for the old Polish officer caste than from any Marxist–Leninist convictions. He had no illusions about the Soviet Union and had no respect for the Polish Communist group in Moscow. They in turn never trusted Berling.

The new formation became the Kościuszko Division, then the 1st Polish Army. In its first battle at Lenino, in 1943, Berling's troops fought doggedly and suffered heavy losses. But in the summer of 1944 the 1st Army was among the Soviet forces which arrived on the far banks of the Vistula as the Warsaw Rising broke out.

Stalin's order to halt the advance was too much for the Polish troops. Some units – apparently with Berling's approval – managed to cross the river and establish a bridgehead on the other side, where they tried to make contact with the Home Army insurgents. But they failed to hold the bridgehead, and had to return. Shortly afterwards, Berling was recalled in disgrace to the Soviet Union and relieved of his command.

By now, the 1st Army had grown to some 80,000 men. Once across the Polish borders, it had merged with the Peoples' Army partisans, and general conscription in the 'liberated areas' brought a flood of recruits. By the end of the war, the force numbered some 400,000 Polish soldiers who had fought their way across Germany, taken part in the triumphant storm of Berlin in May 1945, and raised the red-white flag over the ruins alongside the Soviet banners.

After the war, the 1st Army became the official army of the Polish People's Republic. But alongside Soviet security troops, the army had to fight two tragic and merciless campaigns within postwar Poland. One, which approached the scale of a civil war, was the suppression of Home Army partisans still in the forests and fighting the new Communist regime. The other campaign was an offensive against Ukrainian nationalist guerrillas in south-eastern Poland. It ended in ethnic cleansing, as the local Ukrainians were driven from their villages and resettled in the Western Territories – the lands newly acquired from Germany.

General Zygmunt Berling was eventually allowed to return to Poland, and much propaganda was made of his wartime victories. In reality, however, his contempt for some of the Communist leaders meant that he was trusted only with insignificant civilian posts. The minister of defence was now Konstantin Rokossovsky, a loyal Soviet marshal with Polish family origins who took his orders directly from Moscow and placed Soviet officers in command of all Polish army units. As a symbol of Poland's helpless subjection to Stalinist Russia, he was hated and resented by the more independent wing of the Communist Party. But it was not until October 1956, when Stalin was dead and Poland broke away from its day-to-day obedience to Soviet directions, that Rokossovsky was finally sacked.

In Iran, the hordes of Polish soldiers and civilians emerging from the Soviet Union faced their British hosts with problems they had not expected. Nobody had foreseen the dire physical condition of the evacuees, who often reached the safety of Iran only to die there. Neither had anybody realised how many of them would be civilian family survivors. They included some 13,000 children under the age of 14, many of whom were now orphans. Boys and girls alike arrived with shaven heads, wearing cut-down army boots on their skeletally thin legs.

The first priority was health: to overcome the years of undernourishment and the ravages of disease, above all, of typhus, tuberculosis and malaria. The next priority, agreed between the British, the Polish government in London and General Anders, was to separate the army from the civilians. The troops would be moved out of Iran into Iraq. From there they would be transported to Palestine (at that time, still a British mandate). In camps near Haifa, they would be retrained, equipped with British weapons, tanks, vehicles and uniforms, and eventually sent into battle as the 2nd Polish Corps, attached to the British 8th Army.

But the tens of thousands of civilians put the British in a dilemma. Although food was scarce in Iran, there was no home for the refugees to return to while Poland was under enemy occupation. Neither could they accompany the troops to Palestine, apart from several hundred young women who volunteered to join the forces or the military nursing services. Even keeping the civilians in Iran until the end of the war was thought undesirable. The country was under joint British, American and Soviet occupation, a delicate diplomatic balance which was already putting a strain on Persian patriotic feelings.

At first, the civilians were housed in camps around Teheran. But several thousand children, almost all orphans or at least separated from their parents, were sent to Isfahan. There they were well fed, resumed their education in improvised Polish schools and even learned to weave Persian carpets.

The rest, the British decided, would have to be removed to

distant parts of the British Empire and Commonwealth for the duration of the war. This deeply upset the refugees, who still assumed that they would return to a free Poland as soon as it was liberated. They wanted to remain as close as possible to their homeland, and to their husbands or sons in the Polish armed forces. But the plans for dispersal went ahead, and the families were shipped off to Rhodesia, Kenya or India, to Australia or New Zealand. A few managed to be sent to Mexico, where they were at least close to relatives in the United States. They were to remain in these sunny places of banishment until well after the war ended, hoping that if they could not go home, they would at least be reunited with the demobilised soldiers and airmen or with relations freed from the camps of Nazi Germany. Many of these families, unwilling to return to a Communist Poland, eventually opted to stay and settle in the lands of their latest exile.

It was in April 1942, as the first Polish soldiers reached Iran and set out for new bases in Iraq and Palestine, that the men in one particular truck came across a boy selling a bear cub. Later, they were to become organised into the 22nd Polish Transport Company (Artillery), and – much later still – they would go into battle. But at that stage in the war, almost the only Poles fighting the Nazi enemy on the ground were the men and women in the resistance at home.

There was one exception. This was the Independent Carpathian Rifle Brigade, composed of men who had escaped into Romania in September 1939 and had then managed to reach the Middle East by ship. They had joined the French forces in Syria, but after France's surrender in July 1940, the French commanders at Damascus decided to stand by the Vichy regime and its cease-fire. Determined to carry on the war, the Brigade marched out of Syria into British-controlled Palestine. There the Poles attached themselves to the British army preparing to defend Egypt against the Afrika Korps, commanded by General Erwin Rommel.

They did not have long to wait. In August 1941 the Brigade was landed in the besieged Libyan port of Tobruk. After five months of hard fighting against Nazi tanks and dive-bombers, the Poles stormed a key German strongpoint and effectively broke the siege, opening the way for the British 8th Army to relieve the defenders. From then on, the Brigade was almost continuously in action until the end of the war in Europe.

Back in Iraq and Palestine, making a new fighting force out of the men who had crossed the Caspian was turning out to be a slow business. Physical fitness remained a problem, and there were malaria outbreaks among the troops in some of the bleak desert camps in Iraq. Conversion to British weapons and equipment, and learning to work with 8th Army units who spoke only English, took time, and it was not until the main force settled into camps in Palestine that training really gathered speed. Unlike the Carpathian Rifles, the Anders Army was not able to take part in the North African campaigns, and only reached 'combat readiness' in late 1943, when the Allies had already landed in Sicily and the toe of Italy.

By then, Poland's national future had grown much darker. In April 1943, the Germans had uncovered the mass grave of Polish officers at Katyń, and had gleefully proclaimed Soviet guilt to the world. The Polish government in London demanded a full Red Cross enquiry. In response, the Soviet Union claimed implausibly that Katyń was a Nazi crime, accused the Poles of giving aid and comfort to Nazi propaganda, and broke off relations with Sikorski's government. Sikorski himself was killed in the Gibraltar air crash shortly afterwards. In November that year, the Big Three at the

Teheran conference – Stalin, Roosevelt and Churchill – secretly agreed to move Poland 150 miles to the west, and to let the Soviet Union keep the eastern Polish territories seized in 1939.

The Polish government's refusal to give up these provinces – the homeland of most of Anders's men – angered the British. Anxious not to damage the alliance with Stalin, Churchill's team thought the London Poles were being 'selfish and unreasonable'. The soldiers training in Iraq and Palestine did not know all these details, but the general suspicion that Poland was going to be sold out by the British and the Americans began to spread. Unlike their comrades in the West, these men knew the reality of Soviet rule all too well from their own experience.

None knew it better than General Władysław Anders himself. A fiercely patriotic cavalry officer, he had fought the Soviet invaders in 1939. After being wounded and captured, he was tortured by NKVD interrogators in Moscow's Lubianka prison and was expecting to be shot when the Nazi invasion in 1941 led to his release. Often in conflict with Sikorski and his successor Mikołajczyk, Anders was fanatically opposed to any concessions to 'the Bolsheviks', especially over the frontiers.

The 2nd Polish Corps of the British 8th Army finally reached Italy in January 1944. A slow, often bungled Allied advance up the peninsula had been halted at the defences of the Gustav Line, whose hinge was the ancient hilltop monastery of Monte Cassino. The monastery had already been bombed to rubble, and several desperate attacks up the mountain by British and Indian troops had already been beaten off when the 8th Army launched a fresh offensive in May. This time, the direct assault was mounted by the Poles. They fought their way uphill, yard by yard, over four terrible days and nights until the surviving Germans fell back and the Polish flag went up over the monastery ruins. Beyond the summit, hard fighting for the neighbouring hilltops went on for another six days.

Nearly a thousand Polish soldiers died. But the Battle of Monte Cassino was to become Poland's mythic battle honour for the Second World War, the symbolic victory of raw human courage over entrenched fire-power. Ever since, Cassino has been the theme of films, stories and songs. Sacred canisters of Cassino earth mixed with Polish blood stand in museums. Wojtek the bear, carrying Polish artillery shells to the foot of the mountain, has shared in that immortality.

The fall of Cassino opened the road to Rome. Anders went to the Vatican and was congratulated by the Pope, but the 2nd Corps, after rest and reinforcement, was moved across Italy to the Adriatic coast. There, in July, it led a bloody assault to capture the port of Ancona. In August, the Poles helped to pierce the Gothic Line, and early in 1945 took part in the final spring offensive across the Senio river. On 21 April 1945, the 5th Polish Infantry Division commanded by Klemens Rudnicki liberated the great city of Bologna. A week later, the German armies in Italy laid down their arms, and on 7 and 8 May the Third Reich itself surrendered untidily to the Allies. The war in Europe was over. But the Polish soldiers, who had fought it from the first day to the last, did not feel like victors.

Anders had never hidden his anger at the way Poland was being treated. His soldiers agreed with him. In July 1944, when the London Poles sent a mission to Moscow, Anders warned them that the army would refuse to obey any government which compromised over the frontiers or offered to share power with the Communists. The British commanders in Italy were horrified, and told Anders that as a soldier he should keep out of politics. He took no notice. Soviet

behaviour over Operation Tempest and the Warsaw Rising
that August did not surprise him.

In February 1945, the Yalta Conference confirmed what
most Poles already feared. Poland would lose its eastern
provinces, and would be consigned to the Soviet sphere of
influence after the war. Churchill and Roosevelt prepared to
recognise the Moscow-steered Committee of National Liberation as the legitimate government. When news of Yalta
reached Anders, he sent a telegram to the Polish president-in-
exile in London: 'The Polish Second Corps cannot accept the
unilateral decision by which Poland and the Polish nation are
surrendered to be the spoils of the Bolsheviks.' He was
therefore asking the Allied commanders to pull all Polish
units out of the battle line, to save bloodshed which had now
become pointless.

But Anders did not go through with this tragic threat.
When told that there were no reserve troops to take the place
of the Poles, he announced that they would keep fighting
after all. Something similar took place in Holland, when the
tank-men in Maczek's 1st Armoured Division heard about
Yalta. There was no mutiny, but a number of tanks stopped
and bitter discussion broke out among their crews. Maczek
sent officers down to reason with them, on the grounds that
there was still a job which they had sworn to finish, no matter
how harsh the future looked. The tanks set off again towards
Germany.

All this incited the Soviet Union to launch a hate campaign
against General Anders. He was accused of keeping the 2nd
Corps in arms long after the war ended, in order to use it as a
Polish legion in a new war between the Soviet Union and the
Anglo-Americans. There was a grain of truth in this. In 1946,
when the British told him that his army must be demobilised,
Anders protested that this meant that 'all hope of returning to

a free Poland was gone'. Writing his memoirs in 1947, he ended pointedly: 'We are now living in expectation of the last chapter of this great historic upheaval. We believe . . . and we expect.' Such talk made it easy for the new Communist-dominated 'provisional government' in Warsaw to smear him as a Fascist warmonger. But his old soldiers continued to adore him until he died in London in 1970.

The end of the war in Europe left Poles scattered all over the planet. By late 1945, there were nearly a quarter of a million Polish servicemen and women under British command. In Italy, there were now no fewer than 112,000 men in the 2nd Polish Corps, the Anders Army. In Germany, there were the soldiers of the 1st Armoured Division and Sosabowski's Parachute Brigade. Back in Scotland, over 50,000 new re-cruits had arrived in the training camps since 1944, almost all of them either Poles who had changed sides after serving in the *Wehrmacht* or forced labourers who had been conscripted by the Nazi Todt Organisation. Two new Polish formations, an infantry division and another armoured brigade, had been put together in Scotland, but were not ready to fight by the time of the German surrender.

In conquered Germany and other Reich territories, the Allies found over 180,000 Polish soldiers who had been captured by the Nazis in September 1939 and were still in prisoner-of-war camps. And then, all over the world, there were the civilians. Some, the families who had escaped from the Soviet Union with General Anders, had been parked by the British in India, Africa or other parts of the empire. Hundreds of thousands of others were now 'displaced persons' in tents, huts and barracks throughout Germany, after their liberation from slave-labour factories or concentration camps. And there were the tens of thousands of deported Poles left behind in the Soviet Union, most of whom were being forced to take Soviet citizenship.

What was to become of them all? The choice was simple only for the Poles in the USSR: even in a Communist Poland, life would be heaven compared to Siberia or the Kazakh steppe. In Germany, many civilians freed from Nazi servitude trekked eastwards to find out if their families were still alive or their houses still standing. Others hesitated, while the British – anxious to get rid of this enormous responsibility – urged them all to go back to Poland and rebuild their country. At Yalta, Stalin had told Churchill and Roosevelt that there would be 'free elections' in Poland. The British, without much confidence, hoped that most of the Poles in the West would decide to go home once they were convinced that Stalin's assurance would be honoured. They were not convinced, and it was not honoured.

But this did not prevent Churchill's government from recognising the provisional government in Warsaw on 5 July 1945. At the same time, recognition was withdrawn from the Polish exile government in London, which had been Britain's loyal ally from the first day of the European war to the last. In a final clumsy insult, which hurts Poles to this day, no Polish troops were invited to take part in the international victory parade in London. Later in July, the general election threw out Winston Churchill and replaced him with a Labour government led by Clement Attlee as prime minister and Ernest Bevin as foreign secretary. But this did not change British policy towards Poland and towards the hundreds of thousands of Poles left in Britain's charge.

It would be unfair to see British behaviour as simply heartless. There was much agonising. It's difficult in retrospect to blame Churchill's government after 1941 for putting the need to keep the Soviet Union in the anti-Hitler coalition ahead of the need to do justice to the Poles. Equally, the decisions at Teheran and Yalta to leave Poland in the Soviet 'zone of influence' after the war, ugly and hypocritical as they were, were little more than recognitions of the inevitable.

There was no way that the British and Americans could reach Poland before the advancing Russians, and no way short of a third world war that Soviet power in eastern Europe and the Balkans could be forced back to its own frontiers. Nonetheless, the British were well aware of the contradiction between what they saw as 'strategic necessity' and what they named as Britain's 'obligation of honour toward the anti-Warsaw Poles'. They hoped to soothe their consciences by handling the problem of the Polish armed forces in a generous and humane way. An Interim Treasury Committee for Polish Questions was set up immediately after the London government was derecognised. In effect, this meant that Britain, although exhausted and bankrupt at the end of nearly six years of war, was taking on the duty to pay and maintain and house the Polish armed forces in the West.

In March 1946, almost a year after the war, the 2nd Corps was still in uniform and encamped in Italy. Clement Attlee and Ernest Bevin sent for General Anders to break the news that his army would be demobilised. They added, naïvely, that his men should prepare to return to Poland and vote there, in order to save democracy from the Communists.

Almost all of them refused. Out of those 112,000 in the 2nd Corps, only seven officers and 14,200 'other ranks' opted to be shipped back to Poland. Anders noted with grim satisfaction that a mere 310 men among the thousands who had actually experienced life in the USSR chose repatriation. The pattern in the 1st Corps, previously based in Scotland and now quartered in Germany, was much the same. As for the 50,000 or so Poles still in Scotland, there was little motive for them to go home, and the Wehrmacht past which many of them had unwillingly endured was thought to have made them unfit for occupation duty in Germany. So they stayed where they were.

In May 1946, Bevin announced that the 2nd Corps would be brought from Italy to Britain, with all its families and dependants. At the same time, a Polish Resettlement Corps (PRC) would be formed, to absorb all those Polish ex-servicemen and -women who did not wish to return home. The PRC was to be 'essentially a transitional arrangement, designed to facilitate the transition from military to civilian life' in Britain or elsewhere; its members would be given skill training, including English language courses. The British still hoped that as many Poles as possible would opt to go home, instead of joining the Resettlement Corps, and offered a fairly mean bribe – two months' army pay and a demob suit – to anyone who chose repatriation. But by early 1948 over 98,000 men and women had enlisted in the PRC, of whom only 8,300 decided to return to Poland.

There was a worrying domestic background to these events. The Poles had been welcomed in the early war years as valiant comrades. But by 1945 resentment at their presence was building up, especially in Scotland. Left-wingers, many of them in the trade union movement, were upset by the 'anti-Soviet' bias of most Poles, and saw the arrival of the 2nd Corps from Italy as the import of a 'Fascist foreign legion' hungry to start a third world war. Although there was a desperate labour shortage, the National Union of Mineworkers was hostile to Polish miners entering British collieries. And by 1945 there was a constant flow of 'send the Poles home' demands from other, more middle-class groups, including the churches and many local councils.

'They have overstayed their welcome' was the theme of most of these protests, accompanied by fantasies about 'over-paid' Poles in uniform crowding into expensive Edinburgh restaurants. Also, and inevitably, there was an attempt to smear the Poles by religious bigotry. In June 1946 the odious John Cormack, leader of the Protestant Action Society and a demagogue on Edinburgh City Council, managed to fill the Usher Hall with an anti-Polish rally. Cormack attacked the Poles as dangerous Papists out to take over Scotland, and denied that Poland had ever been an independent state. Here and there, tense feelings exploded into drunken brawls, and there was an ugly fight between Scots and Polish servicemen in Irvine that September.

But this was the low point, and relations between Poles and Scots began to improve again in 1947. There were several reasons for this. One was political sympathy. By the end of that year, British public opinion had begun to understand how repressive and harsh life had become in Poland, and throughout the zone of Europe under Soviet control. A second reason was that the British government grew worried about bad feeling in working-class Scotland, and began to redirect the incoming Poles to England. According to Tomasz Ziarski-Kernberg's invaluable book *The Polish Community in Scotland*, Parliament was informed that by late 1946 there were 36,000 Polish troops in Scotland, as against 72,000 elsewhere in the United Kingdom. Another 52,000 were expected, but they would be billeted in England and Wales.

A third reason for this cooling of passions was that the Poles in Scotland became much less visible. The 2nd Corps arrived from Italy, bringing with them some 10,000 family members and dependants, but their demobilisation took place mostly in England. Out of 161 camps set up for them, only eight were in Scotland: three for soldiers – including the camp near the

River Tweed at Winfield where Wojtek and his friends were settled – and five for the civilians who came with them. Their legendary wandering across the face of the earth, which had begun in Poland, driven them on through Siberia and central Asia to the Caspian Sea, then on again through Persia, Iraq, Palestine and the battlefields of Italy, had come at last to a standstill in exile.

In the camps, the Polish Resettlement Corps gave the ex-soldiers training in several trades, and – most importantly – taught them English. But the PRC camps gradually emptied over the years and, as most of their 'graduates' were transferred south or emigrated to other countries, the total number of Poles in Scotland fell steeply. By the time of the census in April 1951, Scottish residents registered as 'born in Poland' numbered only 10,603 – 9,113 men and 1,490 women. Five years before, the figure would have been over 50,000.

The 10,000 now became the core of Scotland's hard-working, God-fearing Polish community through the decades that lay ahead. On the whole, they kept well clear of the political squabbles which rent the London-based émigré government during the Cold War, and their main organisation was the League of Polish Combatants (SPK), in which General Anders was the leading figure. A new ripple of refugees reached them in the 1980s, following martial law and the suppression of the free trade union Solidarity. Ten years later, after a free Poland entered the European Union in 2004, the ripple became a tsunami of young Poles pouring into Scotland to find work and learn new ways to live.

But Wojtek was no longer there to greet them. So reluctantly handed over to the care of Edinburgh Zoo, this grand old bear had lived out his retiral in reasonable comfort. He seems not to have been unhappy. But his old mates who visited him found that he was always nostalgic for an army cigarette, a slab of cake and the beloved sound of the Polish language. There had been bad times in the war, but at least he had never for a moment been lonely. His Polish visitors knew what he meant.

# Index